Christian BAYA DIAKILEKE

Digital Transformation: A Lever for Optimal Business Management

Christian BAYA DIAKILEKE

Digital Transformation: A Lever for Optimal Business Management

"Experience of the Institut Supérieur de Gestion de Kinshasa"

ScienciaScripts

Cover image: www.ingimage.com

This book is a translation from the original published under ISBN 978-620-6-70147-7.

Publisher:
Sciencia Scripts
is a trademark of
Dodo Books Indian Ocean Ltd. and OmniScriptum S.R.L publishing group

120 High Road, East Finchley, London, N2 9ED, United Kingdom
Str. Armeneasca 28/1, office 1, Chisinau MD-2012, Republic of Moldova, Europe
Printed at: see last page
ISBN: 978-620-8-29532-5

Contents

EPIGRAPH

"The greatest difficulty in Digital Transformation is changing the car's wheel without stopping it".

Michael Dell, Founder of Dell

DEDICATION

To my dear wife, Ngiangalele Rachel BAYA, for her guidance, her unfailing love and her support as my wife and partner.

To my parents : **BEYA WA BAYA NIMBAMBA Daniel and MVUMBI MAYELA Brigitte**, because thanks to them, we existed and for their love towards us.

To my brothers and sisters: Furio BAYA and his wife Kezia BAYA, Hugo NSUMBU, Arleine MAKANDA, Ruth BAYA, Hugor BAYA, Edy NIMBAMBA KEMBO, Bonald BAYA NSUMBU, Deborah BAYA, Nadege MATENDA, Nadine BAYA, Moise NKUNDA, Daniel NKUNDA, IsacK NKUNDA, Fifi MAPOKO...

To our nephews and nieces: Nave NTAMBUE, Henoch, Salome, Nordeline Kimfuta,

To my brothers-in-law: Baby NYONGONI, Olivier NTAMBWE and LUTUMBA, who have brought honour to our family by taking on our sisters, who live with them, as their spouses.

To our other brothers-in-law and sisters-in-law: Nathan LANDU, Rhodesie, Niclette MAYINGA, Magalie LANDU.

To our friends and their wives: MVUENGA Gaby and Francine MVUENGA, Guylain NDALA and Noella NDALA, VITA Chicco.

Christian BAYA DIAKILEKE

ACKNOWLEDGEMENTS

It is the obligation of every student to write a scientific paper at the end of a given cycle of higher education and university studies. In keeping with this principle, we are pleased to have spent the last two years of our Masters at the Institut Superieur de Gestion de Kinshasa, in ***Digital Communication***, for training and integration of new knowledge, as a teacher at the University.

Our thanks go first and foremost to our creator and all-powerful God Jehovah, who has allowed us to add a new course and capitalise on it, despite the many difficulties, especially when it comes to reconciling studies and responsibilities. The completion of this Master's thesis really shows that the good Lord is always on our side.

Our thanks also go to the Promoter and Permanent Secretary of the Board of Directors of the Instituts Superieurs de Gestion, Mr **BUGEME CHIRABA Jerome, Ordinary Professor,** who strongly encouraged us in this initiative.

We would like to express our sincere thanks to **Professor Celestin NIKIANA MAZAMBA**, who made himself totally available for the direction and supervision that led to the completion of this work, even though he had his other occupations. May the good Lord grant him many blessings.

We cannot forget the encouragement of our dear teaching colleagues, who have enabled us to pursue this path, namely: CT Robert KADIMA, CT Blaise BUATA, CT Jules TSHINYAMAN TSHITOKO, CT OTSHINGA Bathy, CT BONONO, CT Francis Kahembe, CT Ficher, 1'Assistant Severin BULAYA...

We would like to express our deep gratitude to the academic, scientific and administrative staff of the Institut Superieur de Gestion de Kinshasa, not forgetting all the other supervisors and assistants at ISG-Kinshasa.

I can't finish without thanking the members of the Management Committee of the Institut Superieur de Gestion de Kasangulu (ISG-KAS) for their close collaboration: the honorary Academic Secretary General, CT MANGA

BUANANDEKE Gerard, the current Academic Secretary General BM NYEMBWE TSHIMPAKA Jean-Claude, the Secretary General for Research CT Pere Alain-Marie CIMANGA MABIKA.

We would like to thank all the administrative staff at ISG-Kasangulu, who made themselves available during the time we took to carry out our research, which resulted in this Master's thesis: TSHABU MABIKA Plamedie, MFUTILA MAYINGA espoir, MASSAMBA MAMPUYA, NDEKO ABILI and Appariteur NDANDU Jose.

Finally, we would like to express our sincere thanks to all those who have supported us, either directly or indirectly, even if their names do not appear in this work.

Christian BAYA DIAKILEKE

Resume

Faced with the transformations taking place in today's environment (fierce competition, technological change, robotisation, globalisation, etc.), no-one can deny that "*Digital Transformation*" represents an essential and indisputable lever for optimising the Management and integral Development of any company concerned with preserving its survival.

This Master's thesis in Digital Communication proposes effective innovation strategies which, individually or collectively, will help to make both the Institut Superieur de Gestion and its staff more competent and, subsequently, to integrate innovation into all sectors of activity, principally those of Education, Research and Administration.

Experts, entrepreneurs, business managers and even politicians, today everyone must agree that innovation is essential. More than ever, it is the engine of growth in developed countries and the key to business competitiveness. But it is a complex phenomenon that seems difficult to master.

Innovation is a process that cannot be controlled, but rather managed. Innovation is a process that can't be controlled, but rather managed. It's brought about by **digital transformation**, which in turn brings with it new skills and upheavals, including for **managers in all sectors of activity at ISG-Kin**, who have to face up to new challenges.

In this Master's thesis, innovation is analysed through the prism of internal organisation and human resources management. We consider the Institut Superieur de Gestion de Kinshasa (ISG-KIN) as an evolving product, i.e. one with a life cycle from conception to the current phase, which we call ***'Maturity'.***

Thus, thanks to the digital transformation, 1 product innovation will correspond to the launch of a new product or an existing product, but incorporating new features, in particular the digitisation of the Library to promote scientific research through online access, the integration of Tele-

Learning, the valorisation of work by staff and the emergence of a new work organisation and the digitisation of the institution's financial processes.

Christian BAYA DIAKILEKE

GENERAL INTRODUCTION

0.1. Context of the subject

The development of new technologies in recent years and the exponential increase in the volumes of data collected and processed have brought about major changes in businesses.

In this digital age, companies have to face up to two main challenges: on the one hand, the need for reactivity in the face of market globalisation, increasing competitive intensity and the growing power of customers, and on the other hand, the rapid development of information and communication technologies which encourage exchanges both within an organisation and externally (Louart, 1996; Kalika & al., 2000).

Faced with these upheavals in the contemporary environment (fierce competition, technological change, robotisation, globalisation, etc.), no-one can deny that *"digital transformation"* has become an essential and indisputable factor in optimising the management and integral development of any business concerned with preserving its survival.

The strong position that digital transformation occupies in the enterprise is mainly due, on the one hand, to its ability to solve tricky problems that require a great deal of reflection on the part of managers, and on the other hand, to its remarkable evolution over time.

It should also be noted that digital transformation necessarily implies the integration of a new management system, which leads us to assert that management is a tool for developing the economic and social performance of the company.

Our field of research is initially centred on digital transformation, which directly introduces

1 innovation. Hence the presence in this work of several management concepts, in particular: management of innovation and management of information systems, with the aim of "*implementing management techniques and systems designed to create the most favourable conditions for*

the development of innovations" (OECD, 1997).

And although this issue is one of the primary concerns of the entrepreneurial world, the research devoted to it is still at an embryonic stage (Read, 2000). Despite the growing interest in the subject, it suffers from a lack of aggregation of theories and results already obtained, mainly in the Democratic Republic of Congo.

This is a vast field of research, which is considerably fragmented and fraught with uncertainty. As it is not our ambition to compile all the analyses that have already been carried out on this subject, we have chosen instead to specify it within the framework of an organisation, in order to gain in relevance.

Thus, our field of research will not cover the macro-economic applications of innovation. The analysis of the general innovation policies of public authorities acting at national or continental level will therefore be excluded from this study.

Instead, we want to focus on the sources of innovation at organisational and managerial level (micro-economic analysis) and how to integrate it into an organisation, as is the case mainly at the Institut Superieur de Gestion de Kinshasa. The organisation as the exoskeleton of a company's internal structure and the development of creativity through digital transformation and human resources management will therefore be our main areas of research. The issues of marketing, financing and protecting innovations will not be addressed.

BigData is bringing new decision-making and performance management tools, in particular the possibility of installing Enterprise Resource Planning (ERP) software.

ERP software, which stands for Enterprise Resource Planning, can be translated into French as PGI, which stands for **Progiciel de Gestion Integree.** But what is ERP? It's a set of management software applications designed to optimise a company's entire supply chain.

ERP software will enable you to plan your company's resources more effectively, reduce production costs and even increase productivity. In other words, it's a versatile, comprehensive tool, even if it is sometimes complex.

This Master's thesis proposes a digital transformation of all management processes, mainly financial activities, teaching activities, administrative activities and scientific research at the Institut Superieur de Gestion de Kinshasa, thanks to the digitisation of all these sectors of activity.

Bringing together a range of functions, this system will enable ISG-Kinshasa to provide a better service to its students through its **Customer Relationship Management**, which is the art of creating, developing and maintaining a privileged relationship with each of the customers for its business), to better control the checkout processes and even to support the institution in production by optimising its manufacturing capacities.

The **digital transformation of** the company is bringing with it new skills and upheavals, and new challenges, in particular :

> Implementing an organisational transformation ;
> Digitising the library ;
> Integrating new information flow management strategies;
> Adapting tools to the needs of students and teachers;
> **Value creation** for a **realistic, real-time view** of actions taken on the ground and
> Convergence of financial flows to ensure rational control.

Today, more than in previous years, the Institut Superieur de Gestion de Kinshasa is faced with a number of realities. Some of these realities are the globalisation of its fields of action, the intensification of competition and the increase in the flow of information. What are the solutions to the problems of globalisation?

The Institut Superieur de Gestion de Kinshasa has identified four key solutions to the challenges of growth based on globalisation:

> Optimise your business processes. ...
> Improve your sales and marketing practices through new forms of awareness-raising that allow you to enrol several

students,

> Recruit and retain the best teachers available. ...
> Manage finances properly.

A successful company is one that has mastered the way it organises its activities and that never fails to keep pace with the times. Every good manager is driven by the desire to succeed. Whatever their size, companies are turning to New Information and Communication Technologies (NICT) to improve their business.

The motivations for turning to New Technologies are seductive. Reduced errors, easier management, shorter working hours, less fraud and embezzlement of student fees. All sectors of the company should therefore enjoy the benefits of New Technologies through digital transformation.

Accounting and financial management play a very important role in business success. If they are to succeed, companies need to put the emphasis on these two elements.

In the past, accounting was no more than a static and historical organ that recorded past events in order to establish the situation and results at the time the balance sheet was drawn up (VERHUST, 1995).

Nowadays, as a result of the management of financial flows, it has taken on an increasingly important role in the success of companies, and must be kept in a special way. However, many companies still keep it manually and carry out their financial analysis in the traditional way, which exposes them to many errors, as in the case of the Institut Superieur de Gestion de Kinshasa.

For some time now, universities have had to manage large flows of information and face major challenges. They are also exposed to a wide range of business issues, such as competition, cost determination, etc. As a result, they also need a set of management tools that can help them make the right decisions on a day-to-day basis. Digital transformation is proving to be omnipresent in solving such problems.

Digitising accounting management will help ISG-Kinshasa to reduce the risk of error and fraud. Automatic data transmission will reduce data entry errors. The software's ability to perform calculations will prevent calculation errors. By automating certain tasks, you can avoid forgetting to process or send data. Finally, back-ups considerably reduce the risk of data loss.

Digital transformation is the process of completely replacing existing manual business processes with the latest digital alternatives. This type of reinvention affects all aspects of a business, not just technology.

Companies seek to create value by implementing information systems that generate tangible and intangible gains. To achieve this, they are constantly investing in information systems to improve performance and generate results.

To support this development, companies rely on IT systems. The growth in this investment has been exponential in recent years, due to the pressure of demand for IT equipment, the development of internal and external networks, software purchases and the development of new applications. What's more, alongside these major investments, the burden of IT maintenance is growing.

However, managers are questioning the relevance and effectiveness of these investments because of the financial burden they represent and the risk to the company if they fail.

In this work, we are going to analyse the contribution made by information systems to business, whether in terms of investment, tools or users, and to explain their impact on the performance of organisations, and more particularly on higher education and university establishments.

Indeed, performance, a polysemic concept, is traditionally lost in a financial perspective where the satisfaction of shareholders, as stakeholders, is privileged (L. Batsch, 1996).

However, this can be lost through a multi-criteria evaluation in which the interests of all the players are integrated (R.S. Kaplan and D.P. Norton, 1996; G. Charreaux and P. Desbrieres, 1998).

0.2. Problem

Today, information systems (IS) are essential to the smooth running, performance and competitiveness of businesses. Every manager needs to understand and master their workings, potential and essential risks.

They need to know what they are, how they influence the organisation, and how they can improve the work of each individual and each team, thereby making the organisation more efficient.

While the IS is an asset in business competition, it is also a highly critical element. Its robustness and reliability are paramount, as illustrated by this work, which aims to optimise the management systems of the Institut Superieur de Gestion de Kinshasa, ISG-KIN.

Every company needs to generate profits and at the same time optimise its management system. The Institut Superieur de Gestion de Kinshasa, or ISG-KIN for short, is experiencing huge problems with the management of financial flows, mainly academic fees, the management of access to the library following a growing increase in the number of students and capacity, the management of staff (administrative, teaching, students and workers), and the management of teaching, ...

In fact, despite being a management institution, we note that the working methods have remained traditional.

For example, with regard to the management process for academic fees, payment receipts are still compiled manually, and recorded in notebooks containing the details of all students who pay.

As a result, it is difficult to easily find information about the student who paid the fee, because it is not known in which document (registration book) this information is found and some students have several codes for themselves.

This situation jeopardises the management of this major process of managing academic fees, given that it is the main process that enables ISG-KIN to generate revenue.

A second case is that of the main library of the Institut

Superieur de Gestion in Kinshasa, which has a capacity of 30 people, whereas the estimated number of students is currently more than 18,000.

If we assume that 60 students can consult this library every day, it will take another 300 days for all the students to have access to it, which will be equivalent to 10 months, i.e. even more than the period planned for an entire academic year.

In the light of the above, our problem can be summed up by the following questions:

1. As an evolving system (product) in its mature phase, what can be done to ensure the emergence of the Institut Superieur de Gestion de Kinshasa in a competitive environment?
2. What steps will lead to the integration of digital transformation at the Institut Superieur de Gestion in Kinshasa?
3. Why do we see digital transformation as a lever for optimising business management in the face of globalisation?
4. How can innovation management be an effective alternative for sustaining innovation?

0.3. Assumptions

At this stage, the aim is to provide provisional answers to the questions posed in the problem.

Since its creation, the Institut Superieur de Gestion has been in its maturing phase.

So, to ensure its emergence, the Institut Superieur de Gestion de Kinshasa must integrate a new type of management, which we call: Innovation Management.

At that point, considering the institution as a product, it will be transformed into a new product. To achieve this, we need to think in terms of total innovation, as a pillar of the company's strategy.

In other words, the implementation of a strategic approach that perpetuates innovative processes within the company.

Innovation has become a major issue in a globalised world where competition has never been so competitive,

particularly in developed countries.
It is also a tremendous source of economic growth, as demonstrated by the parallelism of the curves for patents granted, the growth rate and the wealth generated by innovative companies.
With regard to the integration of digital transformation within the Institut Superieur de Gestion de Kinshasa, the following steps are necessary:

S Digitising the library and automating the library helpdesk with chatbots[1]

✓ Link your data to your processes

✓ Move each course online

✓ Monitoring the student lifecycle, from admission to graduation

✓ Digitise all payment processes

✓ It should also be noted that it is no longer price or product that are considered to be the most decisive factors in customers' purchasing decisions.

And, at this stage, technology is capable of offering relevant changes. Because it has become a direct channel of communication with the public.
It's no coincidence that digital transformation specifically identifies the customer experience as one of its pillars.
It is thanks to the Internet, for example, that customers are influenced more effectively. In this way, they help to build a brand's reputation.
The influence and reach of Facebook advertising and the ease of communicating with the company via chat tools are also worth noting, as they have enabled many people, for example, to enrol at the Institut Superieur de Gestion in Kinshasa.
These days, it's much easier for higher education institutions to stay in touch with their students, creating ways to interact with their brand and better understand their preferences

[1] A chatbot is a computer programme that simulates and processes a human conversation (written or spoken), enabling humans to interact with digital terminals as if they were communicating with a real person.

from the comfort of their own homes.
So, with a digital transformation, your company will have tools that can help, among other things :
Segmentation: Segment your audience using data collection and personalisation approaches, made possible by analysis tools. For example. It's easier to know who your target audience is and what their preferences are. This helps you reach them and attract more prospects.
Customer service: It is now much easier for students to communicate with the company via a digital service than to seek interaction with employees in person.
Simplifying sales: consumers are looking for greater simplicity at the time of purchase, avoiding certain costs and journeys, and enhancing the value of their loyalty. In our case, the customers are students, who through digital transformation can get all the information they need from the institution, without having to go anywhere. Imagine how digital technology influences this process!
Finally, innovation is becoming the best, and in some markets the only, way to remain competitive, to stand out from the competition and to guarantee economic survival.
What's more, we live in a society of satiation, where consumers are expressing increasingly specific and demanding needs. The Institut Superieur de Gestion de Kinshasa must therefore be able to constantly renew its offerings in order to stand out from the crowd with richer content and greater added value. This is why Innovation Management would be an effective alternative to its emergence.

0.4. Lens

The main aim of this work is to enable the Institut Superieur de Gestion de Kinshasa to meet the needs of its clients, in the face of the demands imposed on us by the revolution in new technologies and the implementation of the LMD (Licence-Maitrise-Doctorat) system.
In addition to the above, increasing sales and standing out from the competition by integrating digital transformation is

an innovative solution.

0.5. Defining the subject

As a teacher at the Institut Superieur de Gestion in Kinshasa, we wanted this to be our field of study. This is the area we have chosen to carry out our research and propose a new lever for optimising all the management systems within it, namely digital transformation. Our research covers the period from 2017 to 2022.

0.6. Choice and interest of subject

The choice of our subject is first and foremost to make our contribution to the revolution in science, so that those who want to carry out research on the same subject as ours will also refer to this work.

Secondly, it is the desire to enrich the management system within the Institut Superieur de Gestion de KINSHASA and to enable it to stand out from its competitors.

0.7. Methods and techniques used

We know, however, that research is only scientific when scientific and technical methods are used. To this end, we have used the following methods and techniques:

> **Structure-function method**

This method enabled us to discover the functional structure of ISG-KINSHASA in a clear and detailed way.

> **The analytical method**

This enabled us to analyse and describe the facts and data relating to the subject of our study, in order to make a correct judgement on the data analysed.

> **Comparative method**

This has enabled us to examine the relationship between convergence and divergence in order to assess the management system.

> **Interview technique**

It's a technique that enabled us to proceed by question and answer, by interview in other words, with the people available to us.

> **Documentary analysis technique**

Using this technique, we were able to obtain certain elements of our research by consulting certain documents and reading a number of works.

> **Observation Technique**

This technique enabled us to experience the workings of departments, given that we work in this system, i.e. the Institut Superieur de Gestion in Kinshasa.

0.8. Work outline

Apart from the introduction and general conclusion, our work is divided into six chapters, entitled as follows:

- ✓ Chapter I. Information Systems Management in general
- ✓ Chapter II. The Foundations and Approach to Innovation
- ✓ Chapter III. Presentation of the Institut Superieur de Gestion de Kinshasa
- ✓ Chapter IV. Computer networks and the Internet
- ✓ Chapter V. Modelling the Digital Library Problem
- ✓ Chapter VI. Digital Transformation at the ISG- KINSHASA

INFORMATION SYSTEM MANAGEMENT IN GENERAL

Information systems management[2] (also known in a more restricted sense as performance management) is a management discipline that brings together all the knowledge, technologies and tools used to manage data and, more generally, to organise information systems.

The information system must be organised, finalised, built, managed and controlled, which is a means of optimising the company's performance.

It is a science that is constantly evolving as a result of the new emerging professions in information systems.

I.1 Challenges and developments in information management

I.1.1. Information management issues

In order to meet the organisation's needs as effectively as possible, it is important to create a coherent and agile IS (information system) that can integrate the company's new requirements. But information systems management must also enable the company to take advantage of new technologies.[3]

Information systems security is a major challenge for IS management. Reducing the vulnerabilities caused by the human factor and ensuring the security of the IS itself are key factors that the IT Director must take into account.

Continuity in the event of a disaster has taken on a truly important dimension as a result of the new regulatory standards.

The CIO must ensure that human and technical standards are met in the event of a disaster, but also that organisational management can respond effectively and

[2] **Azan,W. et Beldi,A.,** 2011, " *De la cybernetique a la theorie de la human agency : vers un management des SI cent sur les utilisateurs*", Management & Avenir, n°39, pp. 192-212

[3] **ALBAN D. and EYNAUD P.,** 2009, *Management operationnel du systeme d'information*, Lavoisier, page 29

rapidly to IT problems.

IS management also raises questions about ethics and social impact. Certain standards protect the company's employees, particularly with regard to the protection of privacy and intellectual property. The information system must not violate these ethical standards in order to avoid any legal reprisals.

To achieve this, information systems management must enable the CIO to put in place an organisational policy within the information system to protect data and information flows.

The legal and tax implications of information systems management mean that it is important to integrate and master the legal and tax constraints associated with the computerisation of their information systems. It also makes it possible to respond to requests from representatives of the tax authorities and to provide the necessary information, and only that information.

I.1.2. Developments in information systems management

The concept of "Management of Information Systems" appeared in the mid-60s in the United States and a few years later in France. However, this concept has evolved considerably to the point where it now concerns not only IT management but also "Management Information Systems".

Information system management[4] is influenced by research into system structures and the conceptualisation of decision support at the IT level. At management level, information system management is influenced by the quality management department in companies.

Finally, economists (Robert Solow, Daniel Cohen (economist), etc.) have shown that information systems only generate productivity gains if they are accompanied by change. Change in organisations is therefore inseparable from software. This new dimension means that an originally

[4] **Beaufils,B., Brandouy,O., Ma,L., et Mathieu,P.,** 2009, "*Simuler pour comprendre : un eclairage sur les dynamiques de marches financiers a l'aide des systemes multiagents*", *systemes d'Information et Management*, vol. 14, n°4, pp.51-70

rather *hard* science has had to turn to continuous improvement techniques such as Lean.

1.1.3. Management

Management[5] is the set of techniques for organising the resources used to manage an entity, including the art of managing people, in order to achieve satisfactory performance.

With a view to optimisation, it tends to respect the interests and representations of the company's stakeholders. In order to take account of time, risk and information in management decision-making, it is customary to distinguish between :

S **Strategic** management, which involves managing the market through strategy (this is also an external view of management);

S **Operational** management, which concerns the management of the company's own processes (a more internal vision centred on the organisation).

S Management control tends to act as a link between these two types of management by virtue of its position within the company.

The management challenges are to :

- Manage the organisation's resources effectively.

This requires the use of tools that draw particularly on economics, but also on sociology and psychology. Management must therefore succeed in taking account of the representations and interests of the various stakeholders in the organisation, while remaining focused on organisational optimisation.

- Coaching employees

Over the last few years, corporate coaching has become very popular. But far from being just a fad, coaching can be an excellent lever for more humane and more effective management. The advice we offer below will enable managers to provide their staff with excellent coaching.

[5] **MANSHIMBA Joel,** 2021, *Theorie des organisations et Management*, L1 Management, ISG-Kinshasa, Inedit, page 56

1. Balance your 3 roles: manager, coach, leader

Coaching your employees does not mean becoming exclusively their coach. Quite the opposite, in fact. In fact, to coach your team well as a manager, it'**s important to know how to balance the 3 roles that fall to you**: manager, coach and leader. In the same way, you need to find the right stance for each situation: timing is crucial to the company's success.

For example, typically, if a crisis arises, this is not the time to be a coach, but a leader. You'll need to get the ball rolling quickly by providing immediate, practical solutions. Once the crisis is over, you can go back to being a coach, helping your colleagues to analyse any shortcomings in crisis management. Then, finally, you can go back to being a manager, passing on instructions to improve processes based, in particular, on the results of your individual or group coaching sessions.

2. Show empathy

The principle of coaching is not to provide ready-made solutions to specific problems. Quite the opposite. The principle of coaching is to **give the employee or the team the means to find the answers to their questions and the solutions to their problems themselves**.

Empathy is therefore an essential criterion for successfully 'pushing' your colleagues. When you play the role of coach, it's imperative that you "purge" yourself of any judgement about the employee and try to help him or her, by asking appropriate questions, to understand the reasons for his or her failings or anxieties.

But be careful: **you're not an occupational psychologist or a friend**. You need to be able to provide support while staying in your place (to find out more about compassionate leadership, don't hesitate to read our practical sheet on empathy in management).

3. Give feedback

Feedback is essential6 if you are to coach your staff effectively. Feedback can be positive or negative. The key is to find the right form to avoid putting the employee in a situation of "over-confidence" or "under-confidence". Here again, **empathy is an excellent way of finding the right balance**.

Based on this feedback, you can :

✓ Valuing positive behaviour and developments;

✓ Pointing out persistent failings

4. Set an example

Of course, to coach your team well, you have to be exemplary. That's why management is a difficult job. If you yourself are incapable of questioning your processes and/or your behaviour, you will have no credibility with your colleagues.

Le Roux,B., 2009, *La Transformation strategique du systeme d'information,* Lavoisier.

5. Be adaptable

Finally, **you need to be flexible and adaptable to coach your staff effectively**. Because the principle is that good ideas and good behaviour can come from below. What's more, it's vital to **accept differing points of view and individual choices**. It is by building on these that we succeed in creating an effective group dynamic in which everyone feels they have a place.

To sum up, if there's one basic principle to remember, it's this: you don't grow a plant by pulling on its leaves, but by feeding it through its roots. The same goes for a team.

1.1.3.1. Knowledge management

Knowledge management is really a way of **enhancing, using, maintaining and even developing your team's knowledge**. Not just the skills and knowledge acquired in the workplace over the years, but also all that brain storage space that your colleagues use to read, travel, discover, think about, taste - in short, live. Yes, there is life outside your SME. You should try it.

But knowledge management also (and above all, it's true) means recognising your employees' ability to develop knowledge and new skills in the workplace, however unexpected they may be. Your employee is not an immutable creature, who will leave your company with the same level of know-how and savoir-etre as when they entered.

Your SME is likely to **enrich the professional, intellectual, social and even emotional lives of your team**. It's up to you to ensure that these changes also benefit your company.

1.1.3.2. Knowledge management and innovation: SMEs on the front line

If ever there was a fertile ground for developing skills and putting them to good use, it is the VSE and SME sector, i.e. companies in which the employee often has to demonstrate versatility, autonomy and a sense of initiative, but nevertheless often works close to his boss, in a position that encourages exchanges. We can also assume that, as employees of SMEs are much more involved in the development of the organisation employing them, **their ability to develop new skills will be greater than that of employees of large companies**.

For an SME looking to innovate faster and better than its competitors, this is an essential fact. Soliciting the brains of your employees (if possible without risky surgical manipulation) offers you a unique opportunity to get ahead. But you need to give yourself the means to do so!

1.1.3.3. The keys to success

It's up to you, as the owner of your SME, to create the conditions for effective knowledge management, so that you can make savings or profits thanks to a better-structured organisation, or offer products or services that provide a real plus and significant innovation for your customers. Remember that even a seemingly small or insignificant change can turn your company into a winning structure, constantly striving to improve.

How do you go about it?

- First of all, **have an objective view of the skills of your managers and staff**. Make a list of them, analyse them and find out how you can develop this diverse knowledge (courses, training, *corporate* weekends, etc.), etc.).
- **Also analyse your knowledge and skills**, and make sure

you pass them on as often as possible, through meetings, interviews, or simply by being present at every stage in the life of your VSE/SME.

- **Give your team the desire to go the extra mile**: you need to sell your company to your employees too, and give them the desire to get involved at every moment. Respect their audacity and listen to their opinions. Give them the floor and the initiative, and put your trust in them. Talk to them. In short, don't be like the statue of the Commander, threatening and icy. Be nice!
- **Take the plunge**: if someone suggests a new mail distribution system, a different order management model, or the modernisation of one of your packagings, take a little time to think about it and weigh up the advantages and disadvantages, but don't always say no. The words 'yes', 'why not' and 'let's go for it' will have to become part of your vocabulary. The words "yes", "why not" and "let's go for it" will have to become part of your vocabulary.

Finally, give yourself regular opportunities to **take stock, with your employees, of the innovations that have been put in place**, but also of the situation of each individual. Because a frustrated, under-stimulated, stagnating employee will soon be doing you no good.

1.1.3.4. Agile Management

In an increasingly competitive economic world, both locally and globally, corporate agility is undoubtedly one of the keys to competitiveness. In diametric opposition to the traditional Taylorism so deeply rooted in French business culture, agile management is based on the recognition and involvement of each individual in the implementation of projects, as well as on simple and effective methods for optimising productivity... without excessive pressure. Here's how it works.

Once again. To present and define agile management, let's borrow a method dear to American lecturers: the metaphor. **Agile management is all about rocks and pebbles**.

Let's imagine that we need to move a huge boulder. With traditional management, we'd have someone in charge, the manager, who would say to his teams: "There's strength in numbers, push as hard as you can, and eventually you'll move the boulder to its destination. In the meantime, as you'll be behind the rock, you won't see the obstacles in the way. So I'll prepare the way to make the work easier, and I'll make sure that everyone works as they should... " To sum up: **a lot of energy spent for little result**, **an unknown completion time** and **many obstacles to overcome**.

In an agile management approach, it is all the employees who will decide, around a table and with the manager, how the teams who will take care of the move will be put together. Some will clear the way, while others will break the rock into hundreds of pieces that will be easier for another team to transport as it goes along. **Resources are used more efficiently**, **the result is achieved more quickly** and **everyone is involved, valued and motivated**.

In fact, **agile management is based on a *bottom-up* organisation,** as opposed to the classic *top-down* management of traditional Taylorism. **It's all about bottom-up innovation in a lean logic**: it's the involvement of everyone and the concerted efforts of all that make it possible both to come up with solutions that the manager would not have thought of on his own and to motivate the troops.

In addition, agile management involves **knowing how to break down a project into hundreds of small tasks**. This enables :

It's better to achieve a large number of small objectives quickly, with tasks that everyone can cope with, than to take time to reach a single objective with a colossal task (the image of a rock);

Get a clearer picture of how the project is progressing;

Delivering project sections to customers on a regular basis, rather than the whole project. Customers are reassured because they can see how the project is progressing. What's more, this way of working makes the company more efficient, more agile and, *ultimately,* more profitable, because any changes that are made can be implemented very easily and at a lower cost.

What's more, to encourage agile management, we need to apply a few simple methods that greatly optimise the work of the teams. One example is **visual management**, which involves making project summary tables available to the customer, so that :

See at a glance what's been done, what needs to be done and what's on the schedule;

Valuing everyone's involvement: each task is associated (by colour, for example) with the person who carried it out.

- At the same time, it facilitates daily scrums.

This illustration is found in the last chapter of our Memoir.

Agility is achieved through daily scrums[6] where each member of the team takes stock of what they did the day before, what they need to do on the day and what difficulties they are encountering. Because these scrums take place every day, the team becomes agile: **problems are identified before they become real obstacles**. Together, we find solutions and improve processes on a day-to-day basis.

Agile management is therefore fundamentally based on **exchange**, **transparency** and **the sharing of knowledge**, **know-how...** but also of problems and obstacles encountered. In this sense, setting up corporate social networks can be very interesting.

1.1.4. The management consultant

A young profession that is largely unknown among the managers of VSEs and small SMEs, management consultancy is nonetheless transforming the business world. And that's precisely what this profession is all about: managing change, driving process improvements and guiding management development. A closer look at the profession of management consultant.

[6] **Scrum** is a framework that helps teams work together. It encourages teams to learn from experience, to self-organise as they try to solve a problem, but also to reflect on their victories and defeats in order to continuously improve.

1.1.4.1. Helping companies to improve their performance

A company calls in a consultant when it perceives shortcomings in its operations. **A drop in productivity**, **competitiveness**, **employee commitment**, **failure to adapt to changes in the market or the business**, etc. All these reasons can lead a manager to **call in a business consultant**.

In fact, its role will be to analyse how the business operates, how it is positioned in the market (in relation to its targets and competitors) and to propose an improvement plan that will enable the company to develop methods for sustainable success.

1.1.4.2. Management consultancy: the method

Business consultants are often graduates of engineering or business schools. But that's not all. They have a wide range of skills and must master a number of subjects: organisational sociology, systemic and functional analysis methods, etc. But above all, they must be able to listen and determine the real needs of the company. It is these skills that enable them to **analyse in detail and propose appropriate solutions**.

Because what a management consultant shouldn't do is come up with ready-made solutions that don't really correspond to the company's needs or culture. In most cases, **a consulting assignment begins with observation and interviews**. It is through these that the consultant will be able to isolate not only the real needs (which may differ from the expressed needs) but also the areas for improvement.

Once this analysis has been carried out, the management consultant will propose a plan and recommendations to be implemented in order to achieve the objectives set. Finally, of course, the consultant will support the change within the company. This work can take 3 months, 6 months or even more than a year! What aspects of the company are involved? Although it may happen that one department or one aspect of a company's operations is particularly faulty, more often than not, when a business consultant is involved, he or she is working on a large number of related processes. The information system, the sales department, the organisation of workstations, the relationship between employees and their manager, the pricing policy, the product/market fit, etc. **all these elements can be impacted by the management consultant's intervention**. This is also why a consulting assignment can sometimes take months: you can't change all these processes in 1 week.

Employees need to be supported, and change needs to be brought about smoothly and logically, to ensure that implementation is effective and sustainable. A management consultant is not a doctor who puts a band-aid on a wound: he or she is a true architect of change who will fundamentally overhaul the way the company operates. The idea may be frightening at times, but the key is always long-term success.

1.1.4.3. Lean management or how to boost profitability

Often criticised as a management fad on the one hand, or as a way of sacrificing employees on the altar of profitability on the other, lean management has been the subject of much controversy in recent years. However, when you take a close look at its principles, it becomes clear that lean management has been massively overtaken by a Western corporate culture that is far removed from the philosophy of this approach, which originated in Japan. Because it was lean management that enabled Toyota to become the world leader in its sector. So why shouldn't you?

1.1.4.3.1. What is Lean Management?

Lean' is the English **word for slimming down**. In fact, the fundamental principle of lean management is to 'slim down' the company and its processes by eliminating everything that is superfluous: **eliminating waste**, **reducing manufacturing and delivery times**, **reducing all processes**, **optimising workstations**, etc. Lean management is therefore the very opposite of an approach that aims to relocate to low-cost countries. Lean is therefore the very opposite of an approach that aims to relocate to low-cost countries. The aim of lean is to **make a company competitive**, while retaining its employees and making the most of them!

Lean management also aims to integrate each employee into **a global strategy of participative innovation**. This is because every employee is invited to reflect on the tasks and processes in which they are involved and to suggest improvements. In a lean management approach, all employees are involved in the company's success and its ability to move forward. This is "kaizen": **the principle of continuous and infinite improvement**. Adopting the lean method means accepting that no company, no process, no product is ever perfect, and that they must therefore be constantly improved.

And all with a single objective: customer satisfaction and the creation of value for the customer. Because this aspect is also fundamental to lean: a company must perform to satisfy its customers. In this way, if on the one hand it optimises its costs by "slimming down" and on the other hand it satisfies its customers, then, whatever the socio-economic and fiscal context in which it operates, it will be competitive and profitable.

According to a recent study, companies adopting lean management are **on average 40% more efficient and profitable than their competitors**. Food for thought...

1.1.4.4. Lean Management: what is it not?

But lean management is not, contrary to what a number of self-proclaimed lean experts have led people to believe, a method for dealing with the crisis in the short term. Lean **is a medium-term project to improve a company's competitiveness and profitability**. Not a miracle method for making a lot of money straight away.

For example, lean means rethinking the way a company is organised. Because once the processes have been optimised, there are always employees left unemployed. However, a lean project must provide for them to remain with the company as long as possible, in other positions. In the same way, a lean

project must take account of medium-term support for all employees: from management to the lowest paid. Because let's not forget: every employee must be able to participate in optimising costs, at every level.
So we can see how much lean management can bring to a company, but we can also see what a huge task it is to integrate it into a business. So if you want to move to lean, think about it, but accept that it will take years to bear fruit.

1.1.5. Participative management

Participative management adopts five main principles:
Mobilising staff ;
An active staff development policy;
The delegation of power ;
Any problem must be solved at the very level at which it arises;
Regulatory mechanisms must be put in place (right to error, self-control, etc.).
This type of management has a number of advantages for both employees and the company itself, because participative management satisfies the new fundamental needs of employees (the need for security, the establishment of social links, self-esteem and self-fulfilment).
It also aims to ensure equal opportunities and respect for all.
As far as the company is concerned, the introduction of participative management changes the relationships and day-to-day relations between the various players (boss, manager, employees) insofar as everyone finds a place in a cooperative world, which implies an increase in productivity, given that it increases the efficiency of the teams.
Employees are more motivated, and therefore more willing.
But participative management has its limits:

- ✓ Problems of time and cost;
- ✓ Staff resistance ;
- ✓ Challenging formal company structures ;
- ✓ Inability to adapt to crisis situations

1.1.5. Interim management

Widely used in France over the last twenty years, interim

management originated in the Anglo-Saxon countries in the 1970s. As we can easily deduce from its name, this type of management is of limited duration, i.e. temporary.

It involves entrusting the management of a department or the entire company to an external service provider, an expert in management, for a specific assignment. Generally speaking, directors call on an interim manager to help them out of a crisis situation. The interim manager supports a phase of change within the company and facilitates its implementation.

In this respect, it is important to emphasise that in addition to its "classic" functions, the interim manager's field of intervention has broadened over time to cover a wide variety of situations:

- Supporting the closure of industrial sites;
- To temporarily replace an executive whose absence is prolonged;
- Remedying a managerial shortcoming within the company;
- Completing a project of strategic importance (commercial, financial, economic, etc.).
- Managing strong growth.
- Making the company's production facilities more profitable.

In practice, the interim manager is authorised to carry out his duties by virtue of a valid mandate from the company's directors or shareholders.

This is a professional who has already held the position of director in the past, and who has recognised expertise in his or her field. His or her experience and managerial skills are needed to help the company overcome a difficult situation or to steer a substantial project.

By sparing the company the need to invest in potentially unfortunate recruitment or to draw on its human resources to the point of exhaustion, interim management is the ideal solution for dealing with situations that are themselves transitional.

Today, the use of an interim manager is no longer the exclusive preserve of private sector companies, whatever their size. It is increasingly being extended to semi-public organisations, local authorities and associations. Nevertheless, determining the mission of an interim manager remains an essential step for the company that calls on the services of this confirmed expert.
This means that the phases of the mission must be precisely defined:
Choosing the interim manager: this is the most delicate and difficult phase, since it involves choosing an interim manager whose profile best matches the type of situation to be managed on the one hand, and the company's expectations and objectives on the other.
The interim manager's technical skills and practical experience in a management position similar to that which he or she will occupy during the assignment are decisive criteria for the company, which must also prepare the assignment carefully:
-/ **Determining the objectives and results to be achieved**
It is essential that the objectives to be achieved and the results to be achieved are fixed before the start of the assignment. This will enable the prospective interim manager to form a more precise idea of the task entrusted to him and what is expected of him. If you're going to resign because the profile of the manager you've chosen isn't right for the job, you might as well do it before you start.
Evaluating the progress of the assignment: it is up to the interim manager to ensure that the project entrusted to him is running smoothly. To do this, they need to be present at all times, especially as the progress of the assignment is scrupulously monitored by the managers, who assess the results at each stage. The interim manager must therefore know how to steer his project and measure its progress from day to day.
Ensuring the handover: lasting between 6 and 15 months on average, the interim manager's assignment is, by its very

nature, a one-off one. They must therefore ensure continuity as soon as they arrive, so that their successors or, where appropriate, the company's management, can take over without difficulty.

Originating in Austria in the mid-1970s, idea management is based on a system for collecting and implementing ideas from all members of staff in a company.

Better known today as SMI (Système de Management des Idees), this management technique consists of four essential stages:

Idea-gathering: collecting suggestions for improving the way the company operates is a common practice among business leaders looking to move forward and outperform the competition.

With this in mind, most companies provide employees with a suggestion box. With the spread of the Internet, there has been a proliferation of company websites and blogs where users, whether employees or customers of the company, can leave comments, give their opinion on a particular product or make a suggestion to increase customer satisfaction.

As a general rule, the speakers are left free to choose the subject on which they will give their opinion, but it is also possible to guide them by asking them a specific question about a particular product, for example. This is particularly useful when the company wants to measure the relevance of an approach it has recently adopted, or to find out what consumers think so that it can improve its production and best meet their expectations.

Despite its apparent similarity to participative management, idea management is, in reality, much more a management tool than a distinct form of management. Far from decision-making, it relies instead on a system for gathering suggestions aimed at improving the company's performance.

Assessing the ideas: once the ideas have been collected, they are assessed. This operation is used to determine the relevance of each idea and the added value it may potentially contain. Within the team, the assessment is made directly by the member of staff who has a higher rank than the author. The response time should be fairly rapid, ranging from a few days to a month at the most. If the suggestion is accepted, it can be passed on to the rest of the team, or even to all the company's staff. In practice, it is up to the team leader to carry out the technical and financial evaluation of the idea thus retained but, if necessary, he can call on the services of a team of experts to carry out this assessment.

Implementing ideas: the implementation phase is itself divided into two stages: firstly, there is the preliminary stage, during which the validity of the suggestion is tested. This is followed by the evaluation stage, during which the results of the test stage are used to determine whether the idea can be applied more widely and whether it can become 'best practice'.

When it comes to realising the idea, it is essential to involve the author in the implementation process. Acknowledging the authors of ideas, or recognising "participative innovation", is a key element of the Idea Management System (IMS), which is also based on :

Steering the SMI: Idea management is a process that involves the implementation of carefully prepared guidelines and performance measures. In this respect, the following actions are particularly worth mentioning:

- Calculation of the number of ideas per employee. - The rate of application of these ideas. - The average time required to study the suggestions collected.
- The costs of implementing these suggestions. - The potential financial gains.

In fact, management tends to assess the capacity for innovation and the level of employee creativity, as well as the ability of managers to stimulate their staff and put their ideas into practice. As for the SMI, it aims to achieve several objectives, both economic (increasing company performance, encouraging innovation) and social (valuing employees, recognising their skills and know-how).

I.1.7 Multicultural management

The starting point for the multicultural manager in managing a team of different nationalities is, of course, to compare cultures.

Although this approach may seem too abstract or too stereotyped, the multicultural manager must not overlook this essential step, which will enable him to establish a solid basis for his relations with the various members of his team.

To do this, they must first consider their own culture and analyse how it affects their perception of the following elements:

Time: the relationship with time, also known as the 'relationship with uncertainty', is very important for understanding how people function. In some cultures, the tendency is to control the passage of time as much as possible, while in others, only the present counts, and it's important to make the most of it.

Hierarchy: here again, there are many differences. Some cultures are very focused on discipline, whereas in other civilisations, tolerance of hierarchical relationships is rather limited.

Individualism: this tends to measure the degree of autonomy of each employee, according to their cultural background, in relation to social values or the notion of group.

There are other points to consider, absolutely, if you want to have a complete idea of your team's perception of these essential concepts;

Discrimination: it is important to be able to determine, in advance, which roles are accepted as being reserved for men and which for women, based on the cultural impact of each nationality. This knowledge will enable the manager to avoid making clumsy choices that will only serve to frustrate his employees, creating unnecessary tensions within the group.

Formalism: many cultures are based on a rigorous formalism that makes the written word the foundation of every act, while others are more informal, favouring the oral tradition handed down by their ancestors. Hence the importance for some civilisations of the spoken word or verbal promise.

Religion: this information carries a lot of weight in certain business sectors. Generally speaking, it tells us - or rather, gives us an idea - of what the employee is prepared to accept and how far he or she is prepared to go.

The multicultural manager must then apply this method to the different nationalities he or she manages. This information will serve as a solid basis for organising and managing his team.

The aim of management is to organise the management of all the staff in a company and to develop techniques to achieve this. To do this, it must ensure that everyone's interests are respected and represent all employees, without exception. In other words: managing, organising, controlling and directing.

I.2 Management of the information system

Information systems management[7] or information systems management (also known in a more restricted sense as IT management and sometimes performance management) is a management science or management discipline covering all the knowledge, techniques and tools used to manage data and its security, and more generally to organise and protect information systems.

The information system must be organised, finalised, built, managed and controlled, which is a means of optimising the company's performance.

It is a science that is constantly evolving as a result of the new emerging professions in information systems.

[7] **BAYA Christian,** 2021, *Notes de Cours de Nouvelles Technologie de l'Information et de la Communication NTIC*, L1 Marketing et Management, ISG-KIN, Inedit.

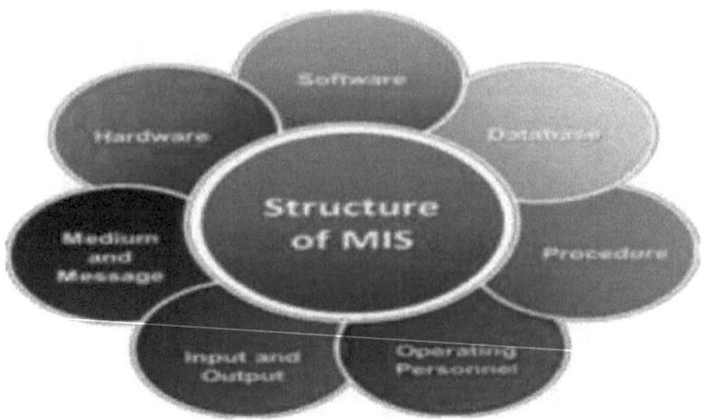

Visual illustrating various aspects of information system management

I.2.1. Challenges and developments in information management

I.2.1.1. Information management issues

In order to meet the organisation's needs as effectively as possible, it is important to create a coherent and agile information system (IS)[8] to integrate the company's new requirements. But the management of information systems must also be able to take advantage of new technologies.

Information systems security is a major challenge for IS management. Reducing vulnerabilities caused by the human factor and ensuring the security of the IS itself are key factors that the Information Systems Director (ISD) must take into account. Continuity in the event of a disaster has taken on a truly important dimension, as a result of the new regulatory standards.

The CIO must ensure that human and technical standards are met in the event of a disaster, but also that the organisation is able to respond effectively and rapidly to IT problems.

IS management also raises questions about ethics and social impact. In fact, certain standards protect the company's employees, particularly with regard to the protection of privacy and intellectual property. The information system must not violate these ethical standards in order to avoid

[8] **Bezes C.**, 2012, "*La congruence pergue des magasins et du site Internet: effets sur le choix du canal d'achat - le cas de la Fnac*", Vie & sciences d'entreprise, n°190, pp.46-70

any legal reprisals. To achieve this, information systems management must enable the CIO to implement an organisational policy within the information system to protect data and information flows.

The legal and tax implications of information systems management mean that it is important to integrate and master the legal and tax constraints associated with the computerisation of their information systems. It also makes it possible to respond to requests from representatives of the tax authorities and to provide the necessary information, and only that information.

1.2.1.2. Developments in information systems management

The concept of "Management of Information Systems"[9] appeared in the mid-1960s in the United States and a few years later in France. However, this concept has evolved considerably to the point where today it concerns not only IT management but also "Management Information Systems".

Information system management is influenced by research into system structures and the conceptualisation of decision support at the IT level.

At management level, it is influenced by the company's quality management department.

Finally, economists (Robert Solow, Daniel Cohen, etc.) have shown that information systems only generate productivity gains if they are accompanied by organisational changes. Organisational change is therefore inseparable from software. This new dimension means that an originally rather *hard* science has had to turn to continuous improvement techniques such as Lean.

I.2.2. The place of information systems in the management of organisations

Information is a fundamental principle of strategy. Consequently, the IS is also an essential tool in corporate strategy. On the one hand, it enables the organisation's employees to implement the decisions taken by senior

[9] **Caseau,Y.**, 2008, Urbanisation, SOA et BPM - *Le point de vue d'un DSI,* Dunod.

management. On the other hand, information systems enable a company's own policy to be defined (e.g. e-commerce).
Certain systems of a different nature have thus emerged to enable the organisation to gain a competitive advantage. This phenomenon is illustrated by cost domination, differentiation or a niche strategy. In the case of the cost domination strategy, the urbanisation of the information system is a reengineering tool that can help achieve more efficient lean IT. In addition, information systems can be useful to decision-makers in the process of designing and choosing the strategy to be implemented, thanks to the collection and processing of information of a decision-making nature. Traditionally, however, the information system is strategically aligned with the company's overall strategy.

I.2.2.1. Information system components[10]

The IS itself is made up of hardware and software with consequences for the management of organisations. In fact, the technological infrastructure of the information system is a set of devices that can bring about organisational changes in a company. These tools are linked by computer networks enabling information to circulate rapidly within the company. In addition, data warehouses are used to collect and structure different types of information with the aim of managing the business.
Integrated management software makes organisational processes run more smoothly and simplifies infrastructure management. While some applications are designed for internal use (supply chain management), others are geared more towards external use (customer relationship management).

1.1.1.2. Information systems and decision support

The main aim of decision-support computing is to assist managers. This has been a key issue since the early days of

[10] **Deltour,F.,** 2012, *"TIC et innovation organisationnelle", Systeme d'Information et Management,* vol. 17, n°2

information systems3 , which can be explained by the importance of information in decision-making. SIADs[11] (decision support information systems) help to prepare and make decisions by providing access to data and testing its validity. Managers will have to make strategic decisions thanks to Business Intelligence and information systems management.

1.2.3. Information systems management approach

1.2.3.1. Change management

The management of information systems is essential in order to deal effectively with constant change. Indeed, it is more difficult in an organisation to change work habits (routines, organisational structure, access to information, etc.) than to change technical tools. This obstacle is the reason for many failures in the field of information systems, since any change can provoke distortions on the part of users.

Cigref (2003) states that "the dominant preoccupation, within companies faced with major computerisation challenges, remains the development of the technical solution, i.e. the IT system itself". [12]It is therefore clear that focusing on the technical aspects of an IS project alone can appease managers by giving them the illusion of control over the results, thanks to its tangible and modern appearance. This reduces the importance of change management and the human dimension of the project.

Yet this is an essential dimension of IT system project management. It is important to anticipate any problems that may arise, even after the project has been launched.

Cigref (2003) specifies that: change exists beyond the implementation of a project, we need to learn from past changes by taking a step back and using examples to help us make decisions, we need to find the right balance by asking ourselves questions such as: can we do without change

[11] **Femandez TORO,A.**, 2009, *Management de la securite de l'information,* Edition d'Organisation.

[12] http://cigref.typepad.fr/cigref publications/RapportsContainer/Parus2020/2020 Accompagnement du chan gement evolution etpratiques web.pdf

management? What are the associated risks? There is no single way of managing change, ranging from the classic vision of "training users to use the new tool" to the continuous improvement approach advocated by Lean, which involves users fully in the construction of the system itself.

Several methods can be used to organise and support cooperation between business representatives, users and IT specialists throughout the project development cycle. Similarly, a number of models derived from management research, including the Technology Acceptance Model, can be used to assess people's reactions to the introduction of a new system and to predict their behaviour in relation to it.

1.2.3.2. Information system projects

Preparing an IS project raises the stakes of information systems management. It is vital to anticipate how the project will run, particularly in terms of organisation, in order to avoid future problems with the project. Preparing an IS project is therefore an essential element that a project manager must take into account in order to limit future problems inherent in the project.

1.2.3.3. Audit of the information system

The aim of an IS audit5 is to highlight the dangers associated with the technical infrastructure and the functional risks of the IS. It covers a broader scope than an IT audit, as it is more concerned with the functional and organisational[13] aspects of the information system in addition to the technical aspect.

IS auditing is based on a methodology known as CobiT, which is the international benchmark for information systems auditing. It provides a number of control standards and "best practices" for assessing IT risks. The audit of information systems is therefore the key player in the control of information systems management.

[14] [13] **Eynaud,P.**, 2010, "*Analyse comparative des strategies Internet de deux associations*", systeme d'Information et Management, vol. 15, n°1, pp.69-95

1.2.4. The information system (IS) [14]

1.2.4.1. Definition

The **information system (IS) is a central element** of a company or organisation. It enables the various players involved to convey information and communicate using a combination of hardware, human resources and software. An IS enables information to be created, collected, stored, processed and modified in a variety of formats.

The aim of an IS is to deliver information to the right person at the right time in the right format.

Interaction between existing systems

An organisation is made up of a set of systems. There is the operating system, the steering system and the information system, three sub-systems that interact with each other:

The **operating system**: this is the foundation of any organisation. It is the system that enables information to be transformed, with the aim of delivering it to the right person. It corresponds to a company's various departments.

The **steering system**: This is what controls and steers the operating system. It is therefore at the head of the information system, setting objectives and making decisions.

The **information system**: This is what comes between the other two systems. This system collects, stores, transforms and distributes data and information in the operating and control system.

In short, an information system enables the operating system to communicate information that has been collected and modified to the control system, which is responsible for monitoring and making decisions.

The functions of an information system

There are therefore 4 main functions of an IS:

Collecting: this is where the data comes from, where information from the company's internal or external environment is acquired.

[15] [14] **Chanegrih,T.**, 2012, "*Les outils de controle de gestion : entre stabilte et changement*", Management & Avenir, vol. 8, n°58, pp.95-115

Storage: as soon as information is acquired, the information system stores it. It must be available and must be able to be retained over time.

Transforming/processing: this phase involves transforming the information and choosing the most suitable medium for processing it. New information is created by modifying the content or form.

Disseminate: the IS then transmits the information to its internal or external environment.

The aim of the IS is therefore to provide information within an organisation that can be used directly by the various players involved and to facilitate decision-making.

The role of IS in a company's performance

The IS has two purposes: functional and social. As far as the functional purpose is concerned, the IS is a communication tool between the various departments of a company and has an operational and strategic role. The social purpose, on the other hand, involves integrating employees into the company, promoting social life and corporate culture through the dissemination of information.

Information systems play an important role in today's businesses, and are even essential to their smooth operation. A high-performance IS enables a company to optimise its processes, outsource low-value-added tasks, improve customer relations, communicate more effectively and boost productivity. If you don't know what your IS is made up of, if you think it's not optimised, or if you want to upgrade it, an IS audit may be in order.

The next chapter will look at the basis and approach to innovation, with the aim of explaining the concept of "***Innovation***" in detail, setting out its fundamental criteria and finally explaining the approach to be followed in order to integrate it into an organisational structure.

CHAPTER II

BASIS AND APPROACH TO INNOVATION

The accelerating pace of technological progress strengthens competition by rapidly demodifying products, and forces competing companies to act quickly. This is why it is necessary to innovate old products in order to generate profits, because profitability is a direct function of mastery of innovation.

There are many forms of innovation, depending on the culture and management philosophies of each company.

Moreover, innovation strategies can be distinguished first and foremost by their nature and their guiding principle. Innovation is therefore the fruit of action by the whole company, under the inspiration and authority of senior management.

In this chapter, we will look at the general principles of managing innovation through its obligations, new product launches and the methodology of strategic choice.

11.1. Innovation obligations

11.1.1. Innovation in general :

Innovation is a very broad term that is synonymous with novelty in everyday French. It is possible to frame this term according to the following criteria. The definition of innovation according to these criteria can be summarised in the following diagram:

French language

Synonym for new.

Economic framework

Criteria

Criteria :

Innovation takes the form of a new object combined with a new way of using it.

Management

It is a new good or service produced on an industrial scale.

11.1.2. Innovation criteria

The ins and outs of responsible innovation are constantly evolving, and will continue to be refined through research and practical application. In any case, in 2013, researchers Richard Owen[15] , Jack Stilgoe[16] and Phil Macnaghten[17] established four landmark criteria on the subject. These are the ARIR criteria, which stand for Anticipation, Reflexivity, Inclusion and Reactivity.

A. Anticipation

All innovation projects must anticipate the various social and environmental impacts, in order to foresee the potential consequences (positive or negative) and, if negative impacts are suspected, to resolve the problem in advance, before any commitment is made to carry out the project.

B. Reflexivity

The aim is to determine a priori the usefulness of the innovation. To be considered responsible, it must provide a tangible and measurable service.

C. Inclusion

The innovation process must not be carried out for the sole benefit and consideration of the designer and the end user, but must include all the intermediate and peripheral stakeholders in the decision-making chain, which may vary depending on the nature of the innovation.

D. Reactivity

Innovation must respond to a real need in society and to the evolution of these needs, such as the fight against global warming, the management of health risks, etc.

11.1.3. Responsible innovation in action

In the case of relatively innocuous innovations, compliance with ARIR criteria may be sufficient to inform decisions and the process. However, for innovations involving a high level of research and potentially major consequences in terms of potential impact (particularly on health, the environment or

16 15 **Richard Owen** was a British zoologist, comparative anatomist and paleontologist who was awarded the Royal Medal in 1846, the Copley Medal in 1851 and the Linnaean Medal in 1888.

17 16 Technology **teacher** English

18 17 English **teacher** in Technology and Innovation.

education), rigorous methodologies need to be implemented, involving control procedures at every stage, and the mobilisation of independent experts capable of assessing the benefit/risk ratio in areas where, by nature, the level of knowledge cannot 100% guarantee the safety of the innovation.

Examples include innovative processes linked to nanotechnologies, genetically modified organisms, artificial intelligence, vaccine technologies, renewable energies, etc.

To achieve responsible innovation approaches that are genuine factors for progress, they need to be based on different levels of perception, analysis and decision-making:

- Documented consideration of the major issues facing society and the ensuing debates, both in terms of the regimes to be adopted in the short term and their future prospects;
- The eligibility of the innovation project with regard to the scientific priority criteria of public and private research and development funding bodies;
- The definition of modes of conduct within the innovation design unit in terms of transparency and ethics.

In other words, the following elements must be taken into account:

Its origin: It comes from a technological advance, a new need and/or a product portfolio situation. Once they have achieved commercial success with their innovative project, companies systematically repeat the process and can then organise their innovation management.

Its role: It has an editing role in the economy. Its factors are therefore considered to be decisive by political decision-makers. SHUMPTER showed its role in the impetus: the innovative entrepreneur, it is through new products, new techniques, that structures end up changing.

Its stages:

1-Invention: The basis of innovation is an invention, the creation of the offer.

2-Business model: Based on this invention, an entrepreneur will build a business model.

3- *Launch:* The physical implementation of the business model: production, purchasing, sales, etc.

Levels of application :

There are two main ways in which innovation can be applied within a company:

- ***One-off innovation***: an innovation project or product innovation is a project to improve existing products, or to create or adopt a new product technology.
- **Continuous innovation:** (in the long term) this is known as total innovation or innovation management, and consists of ensuring long-term competitiveness (sustainable innovation). Innovation then becomes a pillar of the strategy, and a system must be set up to monitor and share information, protect innovations and create partnership synergies.

Its types:

a -^political innovation: it believes in the construction of markets, around which the presence of the state and regulatory bodies is recognised. Conversely, the market is far away, both in space and in time, and the political model opposes economists with a sociological conception of the company.

b- commando innovation: the organisation is the product, the product is the organisation, and this involves setting up a group on a voluntary basis. The commando often drops out of the company.

c- current innovation: the lion's share of the rich vocabulary of the future-makers or the enthusiastic cohesion of the commando spirit, it involves continuous improvement, transfers and borrowings.

II.1.4. Risks and key success factors for a marketing innovation

The commercial failure rate for the most innovative innovations and products is very high, and was 33% to 35% in the 1960s and 1970s for all sectors combined. But the risks vary according to the type of innovation (radical, new for the company or the market) and are more or less controllable. There are two possible sources of risk: product/market risk and company/market risk.

11.1.4.1. *Nature and prevention of risks :*

The product/market risk is linked to the novelty of the product. If it is innovative, it may not be adapted by the market, the market may be too small to make it profitable, or the consumer price differential may be too small.

The risk is that consumers will misjudge the value of the product, weighing up the risk of a trial against the expected benefits. This risk can be of different types: physical (physical danger), functional (malfunctioning), financial, social or psychological (questioning of habits). The second risk is linked to the newness of the product for the company, and its degree of suitability for the technologies, distribution channels and targets that are already familiar with the brand, because this product puts the company's image at risk.

The risk increases according to the degree of novelty of the product on each of the two dimensions. To contain this risk, it is necessary to innovate on only one of the two dimensions. We are therefore faced with two types of innovation in which marketing plays a different role:

- ***Demand-led innovation:*** when a company identifies consumer needs and tries to meet them. For example, in the cosmetics sector, a number of unsatisfied needs have been identified in relation to anti-wrinkle creams, and new products are launched each time research advances to better meet these expectations.
- ***Innovation through supply***: when innovative products are offered to the market on the basis of the company's skills. A classic example is the SONY Walkman, which had skills in miniaturising components and offered a portable player and cassette called the Walkman, which was not designed on the basis of a study of needs and was a success.

In the first case of innovation, we talk about the Marketing function, whose role is to study tastes and determine

customer expectations.
Radical innovations do not come from consumer research alone, but from the application of technological progress. There would be a risk of innovation remaining too focused on the strict analysis of current and expressed needs (LEVIT, 1975), which can be explained by the lack of motivation on the part of consumers, and their lack of knowledge of technological possibilities.
Methods of observing consumer usage can be used to stimulate innovation using ethological methods.
This is how PRODER went about launching the PANTENE brand, using consumer notebooks in which they record everything they eat or drink over a period of time.
Researchers agree that demand-side and supply-side strategies are complementary and contribute to the success of new products. The marketing function is not the originator of innovation; it must quickly take over to transform the idea into a product marketed at a price with advertising positioning. Finally, when the product moves away from the company's traditional markets, the risk focuses on the positioning of the new product within the current range.
The radical nature of innovation has an impact on the value chain of all the partners in the sector (customers, suppliers, etc.) (AKRICH, CALLON and LATOUR, 1988). Faced with a high level of risk, we need to examine the success factors.

11.1.4.2. Success factors and market orientation :

The results of the work of COOPER and others have highlighted that the key success factors converge with the dimensions linked to adaptation to the customer, competitive advantage, associated with domination through attractive prices, with the aspects of research and organisation coming only later. By focusing on market orientation, the authors analyse in turn the role of organisation in the success and failure of innovations, the role of market information and proactive strategies during the launch phase, and the relationship with competitors during adaptation and diffusion.

11.2. Key factors in the success of 1 innovation

1. **Factor 1:** Sharing a common vision of the company's revolution.
2. **Factor 2:** Structure the process and supervise the acquisition of value.
3. **Factor 3:** Create a culture of initiative and open up the process.
4. **Factor no. 4:** Deploy a broad vision of the object.

Innovation is one of the potential avenues of growth for companies. However, initiating, managing and sustaining an innovation process cannot be achieved using 'traditional' approaches, nor can it be reduced solely to strategy, technical design or project management practices. Because of their complex, polymorphic and uncertain nature, **innovation processes require multiple, diversified and interdisciplinary approaches**. As any change inherently generates resistance in proportion to its intensity, it is also essential to put people at the heart of the process.

Let's discover together the foundations you need to put in place within your company, on a strategic management scale, to ensure the success of your innovation process.

Factor n°1: Sharing a common vision of the company's evolution.

Establishing a short - medium - long term strategy for your company is good practice. However, this is not enough to set in motion a process of innovation, the role of which is to give concrete form to your various strategic options and make the most of them in a technical, economic and social environment. In fact, it is first and foremost by sharing the general direction of the company's revolution with the various members of staff that you will succeed in attracting support, and above all in co-constructing and granularising your action plan.

| **The faster you drive, the further you have to see**" (J. Lesourne)

Giving a direction and a description of the desired future is one of the basic precepts of innovation. The more uncertain the environment, the greater the need to adopt and communicate a forward-looking vision. Its appropriation by the players will then be the key to its deployment and its anchoring in the environment.

Using your strategy as a starting point, you need to spell out the know-how to be retained, the activities to be abandoned, the skills to be acquired and the partnerships to be developed. By sharing this fundamental vision with your staff, they will be able to imbibe and acculturate it, enabling you to work with them to devise the activities, products, methods and organisation that will bring this strategy to life.

Factor no. 2: Structure the process and supervise the acquisition of value.

This factor is probably one of the trickiest to manage. On the one hand, a framework needs to be established to give life to the new activity and remove the recurring obstacles to innovation projects (cost, time and persistence in projects that do not generate value). At the same time, this framework must not inhibit the stakeholders' initiative-taking and creativity.

To achieve this, a number of elements need to be put in place, taking care to adapt them to the context of the company:

Defining ways of working and organising teams

Deploying resource management tools

Selecting data processing and decision support tools

Develop a system for measuring and devaluing activity in its various phases. Mark the transitions between these phases with GO/NO GO meetings.

Factor 3: Creating a culture of initiative and opening up the process.

The innovation process is punctuated by studies and actions. The latter gradually enable the value proposition to be clarified and the functional nature of a product to be tested. To grow in the most fertile soil possible, these studies and actions must be able to develop in favourable conditions, which will then increase the project's chances of success.

By opening up the development process to the outside world and encouraging people to take the initiative, the project gives itself the means to be both innovative and to find its place in its environment when it is launched. A number of practices can be put in place throughout a project to enable this to happen:

Test ideas, POCs and prototypes with outside experts, as well as current and potential customers

Organising brainstorming sessions between people from different departments

Be part of an ongoing process of competitive analysis and technology watch

More generally, each employee must bear in mind that proposing changes to any aspect of the innovation process (process, product, organisation, strategies) is part of his or her responsibility, and must feel in a position to do so.

Factor no. 4: Deploy a broad vision of the object.

A common mistake in innovation is to approach the development of a new product 'in silo', separating the different problems to be solved within specialised entities. Doing so denies the complex, systemic nature of the innovation process, and increases the risk of developing unprofitable solutions that are difficult to manufacture and market. We are not saying here that the tasks should not be divided up according to each person's specialities, but we are highlighting the need to think of innovation as a composite triptych:

The product and its characteristics

The associated business model

The technological system needed to implement it (skills, equipment, company know-how, specificity of the product/process pairing)

In this way, it is no longer just a question of thinking of innovation in terms of the "product", but rather of considering it through this trio. Creating interrelations between these elements throughout the process will once again increase the chances of success and the viability of projects.

These four key success factors form the basis for deploying

the innovation process, and can be used as a **benchmark for your innovation management method**, in line with international standard **ISO 56 002**. (V. Boly, M. Camargo & L. Morel (Dir), 2016)

In a very pragmatic way, the different actions put in place can be categorised in terms of their contribution to the different factors present. By keeping this database up to date on a regular basis, you can compare the effectiveness and complementarity of the different practices in place, and so continually improve your process.

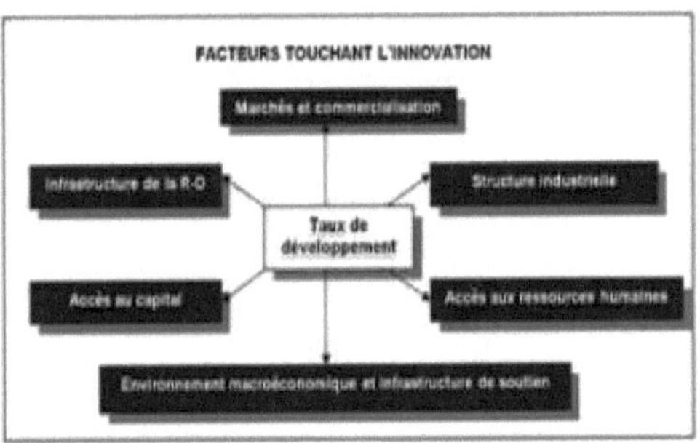

The following figure (Figure 3), proposed by M.GIGET, from the total innovation diamond, illustrates all the interactions that are necessary between the company's functions to activate its innovation process and put in place an innovative capacity that takes into account all the dimensions of innovation: product innovation, process innovation, organisational innovation, etc.

11.3. The diamond of total innovation

Marc Giget[18] defines ten axes of communication in his diamond of innovation. Each axis links one function of the company to another, enabling all the players to interact with each other by various means. The 10 communication axes that make up the diamond are :

1. Product innovation: the R&D department works with marketing and sales to create and design a product.

[18] Marc Giget is currently President of the European Institute for Creative Strategies and Innovation (EICSI) and of the Club de Paris des Directeurs de l'innovation, for which he is responsible for scientific management and training programmes. He is a member of the Academie des Technologies.

2. Self-management, participation and profit-sharing: linking financial and human resources to manage the type of investment best suited to the innovation project.

3. Innovation in the management of research staff (HR <-> R&D): this type of innovation stems from the interaction between the staff and the R&D department.

4. Innovation in the sales force: promoting innovation in the sales force through communication between HR, marketing and sales.

5. Innovation in sales financing: this area is generated by the combination of the Finance and Sales innovation functions.

6. Funding innovation: in the same vein, funding for research and development requires interaction between these services

7. Process innovation: in a relationship traditionally, process innovation comes from the synergy between the R&D and Production processes.

8. Social and organisational innovation: innovating to improve productivity and the social climate, particularly in terms of organisation, is achieved by combining the HR and Production divisions.

9. Distribution innovation: reducing or minimising distribution costs requires cross-functional process optimisation between production and the market

10. Innovation in production financing: innovating in production financing means bringing together financial resources and the production process.

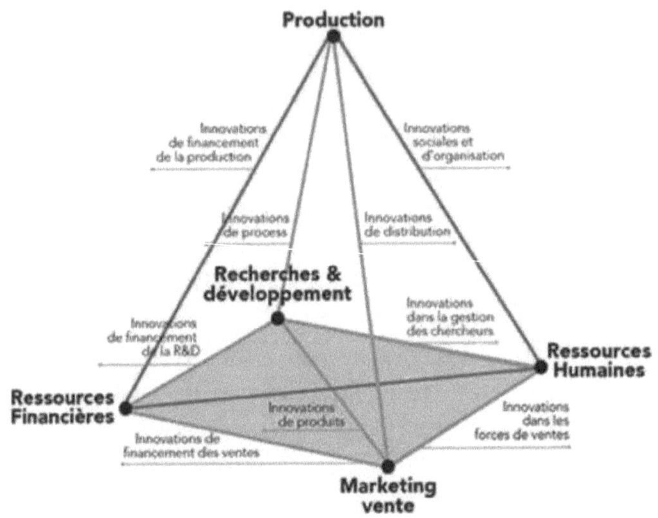

This diamond highlights a number of aspects that enable all possible options to be used to stimulate the creativity and risk-taking needed to innovate, as long as this is not limited solely to the technical or technological innovation of products. In this way, all the elements involved in an innovation process can be taken into account.

For example, a service provided to a given user is judged in global terms - quality and efficiency -. Therefore, any innovation affecting even one element of this service will also have to be assessed from a global point of view. Consequently, if a company that provides a service decides to innovate, it will take care to include the various elements involved in providing this service in a coherent manner.

More concretely, applying Marc Giget's innovation diamond means making a compromise between innovating, adding value and optimising: reducing costs, improving performance, bringing about change, creating new services/products, new investment methods, risk-taking by managers, freedom of creativity granted to employees or internal/external collaboration, etc., with an openness of reflection to all the company's business units. and opening up the process of reflection to all parts of the company.

According to Marc Giget, knowledge should be the driving force behind innovation, because anyone can have an idea and can put it forward. The exchange and diversity of ideas can generate innovations based on knowledge rather than on technology and scientific research alone (often product innovation).

In conclusion, while technology certainly plays an important role in innovation and is often associated with it, we mustn't forget that at the root of every change is an idea.

This idea arises from a need, a desire, a desire to improve or provide a new solution, etc. To successfully implement a knowledge-based innovation project, three important stages need to be respected overall: idea generation (how to define the need, be creative, etc.), conceptualisation (integrating elements of knowledge, technology, costs, services, etc.), marketing (marketing, use of technologies, etc.).

11.4. Launching a new product

1 -The launch challenges:

1-1. Encouraging the adaptation of innovation and speeding up its dissemination :

This adaptation process is the mechanism by which customers become aware of the product's existence, try it out...

Companies understand how this process works, to help them penetrate the market and maximise sales.

Several studies have investigated the adaptation process summarised in this table:

Table II.1: Adaptation process

Le processus d achat	*L adoption des innovations*	*Les hi rarchies des effets*	*L adoption des produits faible effort*
Identification du besoin ↓ Recherche d information ↓ Evaluation des alternatives ↓ Achat et an sommation	Pris de ancien de l existence de produit ↓ Int r t ↓ Evaluation ↓ Essai ↓ Adoption	Prise de conscience ↓ Connaissance ↓ Appr ciation ↓ Pr f rence ↓ Conviction ↓ Adoption	Prise de conscience ↓ Essai ↓ Attitude ↓ Adoption

Main stages in the process of adapting innovations

Launch strategies aimed at promoting adaptation have a threefold objective:

- ***Objective of notoriety*** :

Raise awareness of innovation.

- ***Information objective :***

Promoting information on the characteristics of innovation.

- ***Test objective :***

Encourage buyers to try innovation.

The adaptation of innovations comes up against a number of obstacles based both on acquired habits and perceived risks, which may be physical, social or economic, or based on uncertainty about the performance of the new product.

Adaptation refers to the individual process of reacting to innovation, while diffusion is a collective process and results from the aggregation of individual adaptation processes. Because of the multiplicity of stages in the adaptation process and the existing obstacles. The diffusion of innovations generally gets off to a very slow start. The aim of launch strategies is therefore to accelerate diffusion at the start of the innovation's life cycle.

1.2. Choosing launch targets :

To prepare for the launch, the first decision to make is to define the targets to be addressed (customers). In the launch phase, it is preferable to target early adopters of the product.

The researchers are interested in the characteristics of these adopters, which are summarised in the table below:

Table II.2: ***Characteristics of early adopters of innovations***

Caract ristique socio- conomique	Traits de personnalit	Comportement de
1. Haut niveau d ducation et de culture 2. Haut statut social 3. Mobilit social vers le haut 4. Attitude favorable l emprunt 5. Si l innovation est adopt e par les entreprises : - Grande taille de l organisation - Activit commerciale et sp cialis e	1. Empathie. 2. Moindre dogmatisme. 3. Capacit d abstraction. 4. Rationalit . 5. Intelligence. 6. Ouverture de changement. 7. Capacit supporter le risque de l incertitude. 8. Volont d accomplissement personnel. 9. Attitude favorable vis- -vis de	1. Connexion du syst me social et forte exposition la communication interpersonnelle. 2. Exposition au m dia. 3. Recherche active d information sur les innovations. 4. Leaders d opinion. 5. Appartenance des r seaux sociaux actifs.

They are excellent communication relays, and their demographic and personality characteristics make it possible to draw up a number of operational recommendations for the launch strategy. The impact of these characteristics needs to be nuanced:

* The individual characteristics of early adopters vary according to their degree of innovativeness.
* The speed with which an innovation can be adapted depends on situational factors relating to the intended purchase, involvement in the product category and the way in which the innovation is lost.

Potential customers aren't the only people you need to talk to. It's essential to convince all the players who can increase your credibility and act as communication relays:

* Distributors need to be convinced of the relevance of the innovation in order to recommend it to their customers.
* Business partners and manufacturers of complementary products are also a prime target.
* Opinion leaders (journalists, doctors, etc.) must be taken into account.

2. Time management during the launch phase:

- When should you launch an innovation and how do you manage the time involved in the launch phase?

2.1. The launch moment :

Innovation needs to be launched as early as possible to keep up with market expectations, to avoid trends becoming outdated and also to get the product to market before the competition, but this speed can be called into question on several counts:

Firstly, there is a trade-off between the launch date and the performance of the product marketed, and secondly, first entrants face particularly high risks of failure. Finally, the obsession with speed in the choice of launch date sometimes leads companies to cannibalise their existing products. The company needs to define the precise launch moment, taking three criteria into account:

- Other launches planned by the company: avoiding the simultaneous launch of several new products.
- Launches planned by competitors.
- The seasonal nature of many markets means that innovations are launched just before the high season. Manufacturers use seasons or occasions to present their innovation in order to benefit from the mobilised attention of all stakeholders (customers, journalists , etc.).

2.2. The possible temporal dissociation between launch and communication: Preannouncement

In some sectors, companies choose to announce their innovations in advance. For example, Sony announced the PLAY STATION 2 a year before its launch in Japan.

Pre-announcement has positive effects: it enables the product's reputation to be built up in advance and the adaptation process to begin before the product is launched on the market, which can generate a high level of sales and accelerate the spread of the innovation. In addition, pre-announcement can encourage certain customers to postpone their purchase of a product to await the announced innovation.

These effects are not without a downside: the pre-announcement means that certain technical characteristics have to be fixed while the product is not yet finalised, and it can also lead to the company cannibalising its own products. Through its pre-announcement, the company reveals its innovation projects to its competitors, who try to limit the positive impact of this announcement by launching a new product. The pre-announcement therefore had a dissuasive effect that was entirely favourable to its instigator.

How can a company determine whether and when it is worth announcing its innovation in advance? Several variables come into play:

*Product category.

*The more or less reactive competitive environment.

*The company's position in its market: its market share.

*The innovation itself: the transfer costs associated with its acquisition.

3. Launch intensity and levers for action :

Once the company has defined the targets, the launch date and the means of communication, it organises the practical details of its launch, starting with the intensity and then the levers of action.

3.1. The intensity of the launch:

Mass launch refers to the intensive and parallel use of all marketing tools to accelerate the adaptation and distribution of the product, in order to achieve the three objectives of a launch in the shortest possible time: building brand awareness, informing people about the product's characteristics and encouraging them to try it out. The risks of such a strategy lie in its extremely high cost, concentrated over time. A massive launch presupposes a rapid market reaction that the company must be able to cope with, so it requires significant production capacity from the launch, combined with good sales forecasts. The company runs the risk of running out of stock or, conversely, of having large stocks if its forecasts are too optimistic.

This kind of strategy makes sense when the company has not been a pioneer and wants to catch up quickly with its competitors.

Intensive launches are also favoured by companies wishing to become the market benchmark and whose activities are characterised by network outsourcing. SONY's first PLAY

STATION, for example, fell into this category: massive investment is concentrated on getting sales off the ground quickly and becoming a benchmark for customers.
The alternative to this strategy is for the company to carry out progressive launches, which are less costly but have a slower impact on the market. The company carries out only a few marketing operations during the launch. It then relies on the spread of information by word of mouth and the gradual imitation of initial adopters. This strategy is appropriate when the product category is characterised by a slow adoption and diffusion process, and when the company has limited investment capacity in marketing and production. The risks of a gradual launch consist of slowing diffusion by informing potential customers too late, and being overtaken by a competitor adopting an intensive strategy.

Table3: Example of a massive launch: the XSARA Picasso from CHzoën

September 1998	-Information for sellers. -Presentation of the model and name to the press.
October 1998	-Presentation at the Paris Motor Show. -Customers can reserve the model.
September 1999	-Order confirmation. -Agreement for dealers in Monaco. -Press tests for one week.
November 1999	-Reception of a model in each dealership. -Sales training for regional managers.
December 1999	-Complete sales literature sent to points of sale. -Start of the television advertising campaign.
January - March 2000	-Continuation of the advertising campaign. -Opportunity for customers to see and try out the

car.
-Caps and coloured pencils for children: competition
"Design your own XSARA Picasso".

3.2. Marketing levers in the launch phase :

The company defines its marketing actions on the basis of a number of levers grouped together under the term "marketing mix": product, price, distribution and communication. Adoption is facilitated when potential buyers perceive the innovation as :

S Offering a strong relative advantage over competing products.

S Compatible with their values, experiences and needs.

S Not very complex.

S Easy to try on a limited basis.

S Easy to observe in terms of performance and results.

S Not very innovative.

As far as the product variable is concerned, it is often recommended at the launch phase to market a narrow range, i.e. a limited number of variants: this is to ensure the homogeneity of the early adopters of innovations, and to reduce the costs associated with a wide range at a time when investment is high. When the innovation enters the growth phase, the company will be able to extend its range to respond to a more heterogeneous market.

The name of the innovation is an important decision, and the company can choose between three options: a name describing the function of the product (such as Walkman or Mini Doux), a name describing the positioning of the innovation (such as Avantime or Espace) or a name with no meaning (such as Twingo or Swiffer), which leaves more flexibility for the future.

In terms of pricing, there are also two main approaches in the launch phase: an introductory price corresponds to a high level generating a high unit margin at the risk of limiting volumes sold. This price is appropriate when the company has limited production capacity and faces considerable uncertainty about the size of its market. It has the advantage of limiting commercial risks and encouraging a rapid return on innovation.

Conversely, a penetration price is set at a low level with the aim of speeding up product diffusion and maximising sales. It is appropriate when the market is characterised by high price elasticity and when significant demand is expected to compensate for the low unit margin achieved.

Distribution and communication are also important. Wide distribution enables the innovation to be offered to a large number of potential adopters, but often requires significant investment. Communication brings together a wide range of levers, some of which are used to raise awareness of the innovation (advertising, press, direct marketing, etc.). Others encourage trial: distribution of samples, etc.

Communication based on word-of-mouth is known as "viral marketing". It involves contacting potential customers directly, who have been identified as opinion leaders, to pass on information about an innovation. For example, the first WAP telephone developed by Nokia became very popular thanks to an e-mail message varying its features and promising a free handset to anyone who sent the message to 25 people.

To sum up, there are various levers for launching an innovation, but it is essential to coordinate all operations to ensure that distribution, production and demand are in line, and once the launch has taken place, the results need to be analysed to develop corrective actions. The company must go through each stage of the adoption process and analyse the indicators corresponding to each one: awareness of the existence of the innovation, image for attitude, trial penetration rate for the first adoption, rea chat rate for the definitive adoption of repeat purchase products. Only favourable indicators on each of these criteria will enable it to consider its mission fulfilled.

11.5. The methodology of strategic choice for innovation

Any decision-making process is progressive and iterative: it has to be repeated several times before a result is obtained. It starts with an analysis of the day-to-day reality (simplified to get to the point), measures and compares the different opportunities, and multiplies the contradictory points of view on the issue to make sure that no important aspect is overlooked.

Then there is the interpretation and evaluation of the results. Assessing the opportunities, their costs and their risks continues to be one of the most difficult parts of the strategic approach.

Finally comes the time for the overall decision, the strategic decision. This decision must be carefully thought through, and be based on the first two phases described above, because it will determine the future of the company - its success or failure.

1- Study and strategic analysis of innovation

- Consult and ask questions :

To reach a delicate decision, you first need to ask the right questions. Their purpose will be to help everyone understand the facts, the possible developments, the opportunities and the risks. But they will not provide a single, simple answer. The more in-depth the preparatory work, the more nuanced the answers will be, and the following is a model set of questions that may be useful in this phase:

This is where major innovation comes in:

Solving a major business problem: **defensive innovation.**

Ensuring growth in the years ahead and staying ahead of the competition (first-move strategies): **Offensive innovation**.

Doing what the competition is doing: **imitative innovation.**

Responding to an opportunity that won't present itself again: **Innovation in opportunism**.

Making the most of a scientific or technological advance known elsewhere, by acquiring a patent: **Technological intelligence innovation** .

What the innovation can focus on :

- ✓ On the products manufactured and their design.
- ✓ On the machines.
- ✓ On new materials to be transformed.

✓ On know-how, on the organisation of production and subcontracting...

Means that can be used:

✓ Making the most of an internal resource.

✓ Purchase of patents.

✓ Purchase of external advice.

✓ Implementation of a training programme.

✓ Purchase of materials/machinery incorporating new technologies.

✓ Hiring of a technician to provide expertise.

Real opportunities for change:

✓ With the technology available.

✓ With the company's material structure.

✓ With the solvency of customers.

✓ With the degree of willingness of employees and the company's partners...

11.6. The main phases in a company's life cycle

Every company, whatever its form or structure, is an evolving system with a life cycle, just as Man, as a system, also has a life cycle, from conception to death.

By the way, the five main phases in a company's life cycle are as follows:

Phase I: The company project

Phase II: Creation or launch

Phase III: The development gap

Phase IV: Growth

Phase V: Maturity

Phase VI: Mortality management and restoration.

Phase 1: The company project.

✓ The product does not actually exist;

✓ We make plans;

✓ We have no experience of product management

Phase 2: Creation or launch

✓ The product goes from the objective on paper to a first attempt at realisation (prototype).

✓ Innovation can be high-tech, but it remains relatively simple.

✓ The company needs more money, with a very high level of risk.

Phase 3: The development gap

✓ This is the crucial period in the life of the product, when it is in the middle of its growth phase.

✓ Capital requirements are growing faster than cash inflows.

✓ There is always a gap (pit) between the hopes of success itself (unexpected delays and unfulfilled sales).

Phase 4: Growth.

✓ The positive results have finally arrived.

✓ They have increased the market.

✓ We need to invest quickly to meet demand.

Phase 5: Maturity

✓ The maturity phase is when sales of the product begin to stabilise after rapid growth.

✓ So the product has found its place and sales have peaked.

Phase 6: Mortality management and restoration.

✓ The market is saturating.

✓ You know your job, but it's hard to challenge yourself.

✓ We generate more money than we need to grow our business.

11.6.1. The technology life cycle model

What happens with products also happens with technologies. We can therefore apply the life cycle model to many aspects of human organisations, and to technology projects in particular.

Depending on the degree of technological maturity of the production process, it is possible to produce in small batches (assembly-line production) or using continuous technology, which combines maximum standardisation of components with increasing complexity and differentiation of finished products. That said, technologies can be divided into distinct categories, as follows:

Standard technologies: These are technologies that are widely used by all companies. They are compulsory for everyone, but are no longer an object of competitive differentiation.

§ ***Key technologies:*** are those which today determine the differences and competitive advantages of a company in relation to its competitors.

The technologies of the future: These are a vast basket of concepts that profoundly alter the balance of power between companies, to the benefit of those who master them, if these technologies prove applicable.

11.6.2. The strategic choice of innovation

2.1. Deciding on a strategy

When the strategies of repositioning, modernising old items in the range and extending the range have not achieved the objectives set by the company and no longer guarantee its development and survival, given changes in demand and competition, the marketing manager must consider launching a product that will create a new market.

So, before embarking on a long, costly and risky innovation strategy, it is in the company's interest to study other strategies for accessing innovation, such as : cooperation agreements with other companies (alliances, partnerships), external growth through acquisition or shareholding in companies with product projects or a high-performance R&D department, subcontracting research to private or public research bodies, purchasing patents, manufacturing under licence or franchise agreements.

2.2. Types of innovation strategies

- ***Innovation strategy :***

Companies can opt for an imitation strategy by "copying" an innovative product that has just been launched by an innovative company. In this case, they will not benefit from the temporary monopoly rents enjoyed by innovators: Sony, for example, knew that it could not prevent its famous Walkman from being copied. Not surprisingly, within three years of the Walkman's appearance in 1979, imitators had captured 80% of the market created by Sony.

So, in order to stem the decline in its market share, Sony chose to fight not on price or marketing investment, but by multiplying the number of products offered to customers. Sony put around 170 versions of the original model on the market, two or three times as many as its competitors. By adapting its products to the needs of a wide range of customers, Sony was able to outstrip its rivals and take the market lead with a 40% share, a very high figure in such a competitive sector.

On the other hand, the company will avoid the risks involved in getting an innovative product off the ground and, thanks to a judicious positioning strategy, will be able to catch up very quickly with the leading innovator, especially if the latter is small and has too limited a financial base to erect barriers to entry (reputation, image, cost domination, etc.).

- ***The incremental innovation strategy:***

Incremental innovation is a strategy that does not lead to the creation of genuinely new products and markets. It involves making improvements to existing products. When a company adopts this strategy for one of its products, it is referred to as an adoption strategy. Consumers regard most of these differentiating innovations as false innovations.

In fact, for customers, product and service (the improvement made to a product) are two sides of the same coin. For manufacturers, product and service offer many opportunities to bring value to the customer and gain competitive advantage through differentiation.

Most managers are well aware of the risks associated with poor service. It is estimated that 70% of consumers who are unhappy with a product do not bother to complain. So you have to improve the product and provide after-sales service.

- ***The disruptive innovation strategy*** :

It is at the origin of truly innovative products. It is generally the result of research and development, very rarely of marketing research. The innovative product fulfils either a function previously performed by another product (for example, the DVD compared with the video cassette or CD-ROM), or an entirely new function (for example, the multimedia computer).

In the first case, the company develops in a substitute market for an existing main market, by pursuing a replacement product strategy.

In the second case, it creates a new complementary market (for example, the Webcam market to complement the multimedia computer market) or a combination (innovative product X new market) in which it will benefit from the advantages of legal protection (through patenting) and monopoly, even if they are only temporary.

CHAPTER III

PRESENTATION OF THE INSTITUT SUPERIEUR DE GESTION DE KINSHASA

111.1. The name

Our institute is called Hnstitut Superieur de Gestion, or ISG for short. It was created on the initiative of Professor BUGEME CHIRABA Jerome, who was Head of Studies at thc time, in December 2005, and is now an Ordinary Professor, appointed by Ministerial Order.

111.1.2. Headquarters

The Institut Superieur de Gestion, or ISG for short, is located on Avenue Benseke n°10, in the Commune of NGALIEMA, Quartier Macampagne.

111.1.3. Aims and objectives

The aim of the institution is to provide higher education in :

- Social Assistance and Human Resources Management ;
- Community Development and Population Management ;
- Marketing and Business Management ;
- Business Management ;
- Office Accounting and Asset Management Secretariat ;
- Management Information Systems.

The ISG's objectives include:

- Higher education for intellectuals in the above-mentioned fields;
- Retraining public and private sector personnel in the above areas;
- Raising awareness among intellectuals of the importance of professional specialisation, through activities, conferences and days of reflection.

111.1.4. Organisation

111.1.4.1. Administrative organisation

The ISG bodies are :

- The Board of Directors ;
- The management committee ;
- Academic and scientific staff ;

> Administrative staff ;

> Workers.

111.1.4.2. The Board of Directors

It is made up of a chairman, two vice-chairmen and five members.

Functions	Names and post-names	Positions held elsewhere
President	Mr. NYAMABO	General Counsel Emeritus
1st vice-president	Colonel KELO	FARDC/Colonel
2nd vice-president	Lieutenant-Colonel RUNGUEZI KUNGU	FARDC/ Lieutenant-colonel
Members	Mr. MBOKOLO	AED Director
	Ms Tulumuni Switzerland	Nurse at the Nganda Centre
	Mr.BUGEME CHIRABA	Permanent Secretary

III.1.4.3. The management committee

Functions	Names and post-names	Studies carried out
Managing Director and Professor	Mr.BALENGANA VUBU Edgard	Licenced in DECO
General Secretary Academic	Mr. DIAMPASI SAMBA ZEBEDEE	Degree in commercial scienceand financial (PhD student)
General Secretary administrative	Mr.KABOBO KINGOMA	Licencieen IT
Budget administrator	Ms KOLA KITENGE MAMIE	Licencieen IT

N.B.: The equivalent grade for academic and administrative secretaries-general is Head of Division (CD), whereas for headteachers it is Director.

111.1.4.4. Administrative staff

a) The Chief Executive's Office

1	Chief of Staff	Miss Edith EWUME	C.B
2	Deputy Chief of Staff	Miss MAMIE MBIYE	C.B
3	Legal advisor	Mr KONGA Welcome	C.B
4	Academic advisor	Mr. BAYA DIAKILEKE Christian	C.B

5	Social adviser	Mr. NOËL BAIYA TSHILOMBO	C.B
6	Mission manager	Mr. Mignon BADJEKATE	C.B

b) The SGAC Cabinet

7	Assistant to the academic general secretary	KABONGO MWANDWE ABDON KARIM	C.B

c) The SGAD Cabinet

8	Assistant to the Administrative Secretary General	Miss Tristane MAKELA	C. B

d) The budget administrator's office

9	Assistant to 1'AB	Miss Ruth SEMBO	C.B
10	Sports Assistant	Mr Mignon BADJEGATE	C.B
11	Intendant	Vacancies	C.B

e) University chaplains

12	Catholic Aumdnier	Mrl ' AbbeAlain-Marie CIMANGA MABIKA	C. B
13	Protestant Aumdnier	Reverend Pastor NDUMBU	C. B
14	Charismatic Aumdnier	Reverend Pastor BWANA MOYA SENDWE	C. B
15	Aumdnier Muslim	Mr. NDANGANA	C. B

- Academic and scientific staff

- Academic staff

1. Professor, BUGEME CHIRABA Jerome, Doctor of Sociology ;
2. Professor MAYALA, Doctor of Sociology and Anthropology
3. Professor ALEXIS BRUNO TSHIBALALA, Doctor of Philosophy
4. Professor MANYA OMALOWEE, Doctor in SPA
5. Professor ONGEMBE DAVID, Doctor of Philosophy
6. Professor NGWEYE MAPETO PAULIN GABIN, Doctor of Economics
7. Associate Professor, BUDJOKO IYOLO ACHILE, Doctor of Education

8. Professor Ms KAMONI MWANZA GABRIELLE, Doctor of Education
9. Professor associate KITONDUA LUBANZADIO, Doctor of Computer Science
10. Professor Celestin NIKIANA, Doctor of Law Human and Environmental Sciences.
11. Professor Joël MANSHIMBA, Doctor of Science Economics and Management.

- **Scientific staff**
- **Foremen**

Functions	Names and post-names	Studies carried out
CT	Mr. MANGA BUANANDEKE Gerard	Degree in Science Politicsand Administrative
CT	Mr. DIAMPASI SAMBA ZEBEDEE	Degree in comm. sciences and fin.
CT	KILAPI	Dismissed in Assistance Social
CT	Mr. BAYA CHRISTIAN	Licencieen Computing,in Physical and Cybercrime Expert
CT	Robert KADIMA	Degree in Management
CT	Mr. Jules TSHINYAMA TSHITOKO	Degree in Business Informatics
CT	Mr. Faustin KABUNDA	Degree in Secretarial Technique and Management.
CT	Mr. Blaise BUATA	Degree in Business Informatics
CT	Mr. ALAMBI BONONO Fisher	Degree in Business Informatics
CT	Mr. Bathy OTSHINGA	Degree in Marketing and Experten Communication

- 2nd term assistants

N°	Functions	Names and post-names	Studies carried out
1	ASS.	Papy MAWESI MUHUYA	Licencieen Marketing

2	ASS.	Horso MANZILA	Licencieen Philosophyand Social Assistance
3	ASS.	FAMA YOUYOU	Licencieen Sciences
			Commercial and Administrative
4	ASS.	Grace KANKU	Degree inat Community Development
5	ASS.	LANDU NATHAN Nathan	Computer at science graduate
6	ASS.	Dairan	Degree in Law
7	ASS.	Yves BOSANGE BOKOMBA	Redundant at Marketing
8	ASS.	NGINDU MAGOMBO	Computer at science graduate
9	ASS.	BONGOMBALA OMAR	Licensed as a PSO
10	ASS.	TUTALA DIMEMENE	Licentiate inat international relations
11	ASS.	LUEMBA PHILIPPE	Licentiate inat international relations
12	ASS.	MATE TOBOSO BUCKET	Bachelor's at degree in economics
13	ASS.	BOLAKI MBOMBA	Bachelor's at degree in economics
14	ASS.	LEMBA NSIMBA	Agricultural at engineer

- Heads of section

1. Mr. MANGA BUANANDEKE Gerard, Social Assistance and Human Resources Management
2. Mr. Fiston BENSENGE, Community Development and

Population Management

3. Mr. Bathy OTSHINGA, Business Management and Administration

4. Mr. Bathy OTSHINGA, Marketing and Business Management

5. Mr. TSHINYAMA TSHITOKO Jules, IT Management

6. Mr. Faustin KABUNDA, Accounting Secretary and Office Asset Management

7. Mr. Daniel KABOMBO, Health Sciences Department

- Professional practice charges

N°	Names and post-names	Functions	Grade
1	Assistant Fidele MABAYA	PPC	ATB1
2	MAYAZOLA MAURICE	Driver	ATB2
3	Mignon BADJEGATE	Mail load	CB
4	WONDA	Sentinel	Bailiff

These are directly dependent on the ISG, which has dual responsibility for higher education, universities and scientific research.

III.2 General organisation chart

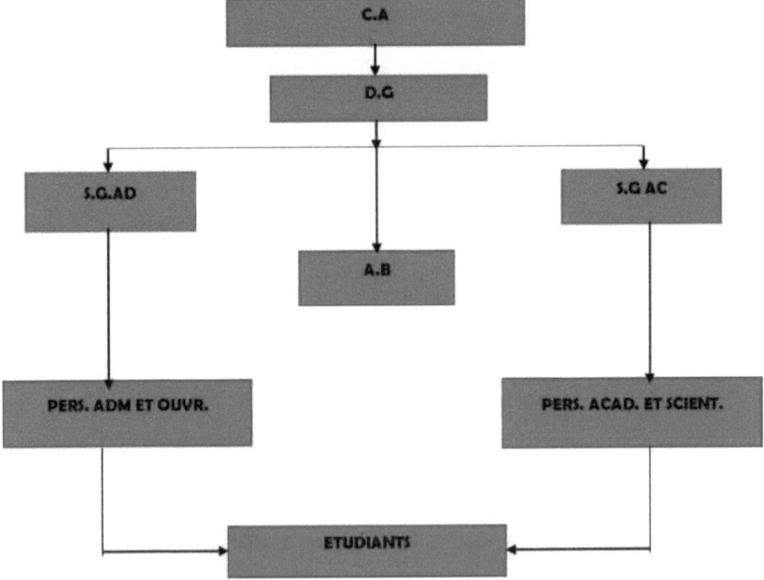

III .2.1. Job descriptions

- **Board of Directors (BOD):** The BOD meets in extraordinary session at the request of the Management Committee, at the Institute or elsewhere. It is the Institute's highest governing body.
- **Director General (D.G.):** This is the head of the school, with the following prerogatives: proposing the appointment of members of the management committee and their dismissal. Proposing the appointment or engagement of teachers and supervisors to the Board of Governors, and their dismissal.
- **Budget Administrator (A.B):** This person is responsible for finance, keeping the Institute's accounts on a daily basis and keeping the Director General informed. She manages the Institute's tax collectors, cashiers, accountant and auditors.
- **Administrative Secretary General (S.G.AD):** Responsible for administration. He keeps the Institute's documents on a daily basis. He handles correspondence. He manages the Institute's assets and administrative and manual staff.
- **Academic Secretary General (S.G.AC):** Responsible for teaching, he oversees the implementation of the course programme and other activities of the institute. He organises scientific conferences and seminars in accordance with the academic calendar.
- **Administrative and manual staff:** are responsible for technical activities.
- **Academic and scientific staff:** responsible for teaching and research.
- **Students:** Are enrolled to be trained by the teaching staff and are obliged to pay the fees set by the authorities.

IV I.2.2. Analysis, criticism and proposed solutions

IV.1.1.1. 1. Introduction

In this section, we will analyse the information system of the Hnstitut Superieur de Gestion de Kinshasa ISG-KIN. The lack of a web platform makes communication between staff in the various offices difficult.

Study of existing facilities

The Institut Superieur de Gestion uses two methods of

communication, one traditional and the other modern but unprofessional.

In addition, we will show that the process of managing academic fees is still manual, and at the same time a hobby.

The ISG organises IT Management as one of its sections, but has no computerised management system capable of handling this process.

Criticism of the existing system

At the end of the communication study or the preliminary study, a critique must be made to show the need for company information. The result of the latter was :

On the positive side

> An atmosphere of serenity among the Institute's staff;

> A perfect partnership;

> Ventilation, environmental ownership;

> From an IT point of view, the ISG uses an IT firewall that is not adapted to several services, as recommended by the LMD system and globalisation.

> The communication system is generally traditional

On the negative side

> As far as the flow of information is concerned, it doesn't work as it should;

> From the critical point of view of the organisational chart, there's not really much to report because the agents communicate with each other;

> From an IT point of view, the institute uses a word-of-mouth communication system, which involves making several trips to get information to its recipient.

> As far as the financial management process is concerned, nothing has yet been digitised, and there is no IT system for managing students' tuition fees. These are the causes of fraud in the payment of tuition fees.

> The lack of a library adapted to the capacity of the school

IV.1.1.2. 2. Proposed solutions

After critiquing the existing system, we propose to examine possible solutions that will enable us to improve the system under study.

The ideal solution, which will both meet the needs of students and staff and help optimise the management of the Institut Superieur de Gestion, is to implement digital transformation.

So why do we need to number the Institut Superieur de Management of Kinshasa?

Every year, new students enter university or the grandes écoles with a huge expectation: to have an unforgettable experience, both academically and socially. Whether they are on a scholarship, paying their own university tuition fees or avoiding the sometimes exorbitant annual cost of a school, they expect the best possible level of education. In this respect, students become veritable '**customers**': a dissatisfied student therefore runs the risk of an institution losing other students and having a negative impact on its reputation and therefore its income.

The new generations of students arriving on the benches of universities and grandes ecoles all have one thing in common: they have been cradled by digital technology. These "digital natives" or "millenials" can't imagine for a single second that institutions are not adapting to their uses and behaviour. To ensure that they don't drop out before graduating, educational establishments have no choice: they have to be digital too.

With the rise of mobile devices (laptops and tablets), students expect all the resources they need to be accessible online and downloadable, on the device of their choice, whenever and wherever they are. They want to be able to keep all the course materials on their device, thus lightening both their backpacks and their timetables, which are freed up from tedious constraints so that they can concentrate on the reason they are here: learning and training. The consequences for the schools are immediate: positive brand image, improved profits with increased enrolments, and consequent gains in reputation and income.

It is therefore essential, as in the professional world, to offer them an accessible space in which to back up their documents and store them in complete security. Because without a viable storage solution available to them, they are inclined to resort to their own means, and therefore to use the public cloud, whose sharing and collaboration functions they are familiar with.

With data accessible anywhere, at any time and via the terminal of their choice, cloud storage meets the needs of students' flexible lifestyles, freeing them from the responsibility of storing their work. Just as in their personal lives, they are able to be reliably connected at all times, whether they're searching the internet, collaborating on a project in the cloud or streaming a lecture. All this on the basis of a secure and reliable system that keeps the school's data completely confidential, and is powerful enough to guarantee continuous service.

CHAPTER IV

COMPUTER NETWORKS AND THE INTERNET

V V.1 Definitions

A network, in the general sense of the word, is a set of objects or people interconnected with each other, enabling elements to be circulated between them according to well-defined rules (protocols).

A computer network is a set of computers and terminals interconnected to exchange digital information, using physical lines (cable, optical fibre, etc.) or hertzian waves to exchange digital data.

S If the link is a physical link (cable, optical fibre, etc.), it is referred to as a fixed network.

S If the link is in the form of Hertzian waves, it is referred to as a wireless network.

Networking is the use of tools and tasks to connect computers so that they can share resources.

The various components of a network can be connected using permanent links such as cables, but also via public telecommunications networks, such as the telephone network.

The dimensions of these networks vary greatly, from local networks linking a few elements in a single building, to groups of computers installed over a large geographical area.

Computer networks enable users to communicate with each other and transfer information. These data transmissions may involve the exchange of messages between users, remote access to databases or file sharing.

VI .2. Network topologies

A topology is the way in which a network is cabled. The topology in a computer network is chosen according to the environment, the architecture (buildings, etc.) and the technical debit requirements of the company.

There are 3 main topologies in the world of cable networks: bus, star and ring topologies.

VII 2.1. Bus topology

In a BUS topology, all the nodes in the network are linked

together in a chain. At each end of the BUS, a termination plug is placed, signifying that the network is terminated.

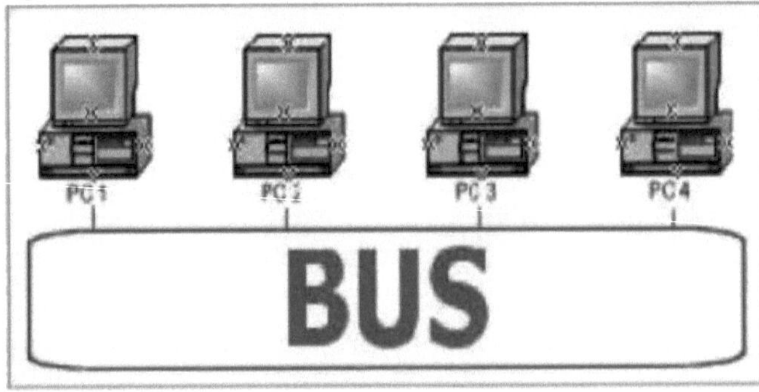

Fig.IV1: Bus topology.

A single station transmits on the bus. When this station transmits, the frame travels along the entire bus until it reaches the recipient. The big problem with this topology is that if one of the nodes is "temporarily" disconnected from the network, the whole network goes down.

IV.2.2. Ring topology

The stations on the network can only communicate when they have the token. The token is intercepted by the station wishing to send or receive frames.

A single station can do "cause" in the same amount of time.

In FDDI, there is a second backup loop in case the first loop is temporarily unusable.

There are two main technologies using this system. IBM's Token Ring, its evolution HSTR (High Speed Token Ring) and FDDI (Fiber Distributed Data Interface).

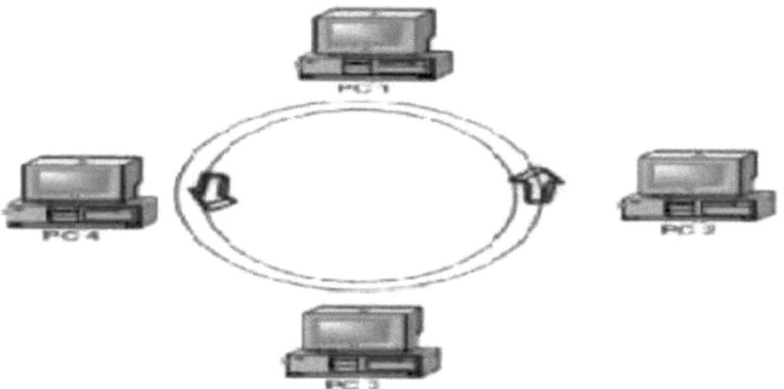

Fig.IV.2: Ring topology.

IV.2.3. Star topology

The system relies on a central piece of equipment (the concentrator or hub) to direct all the connections. If the hub fails, the network is unavailable. On the other hand, a station can be removed without the whole network going down.

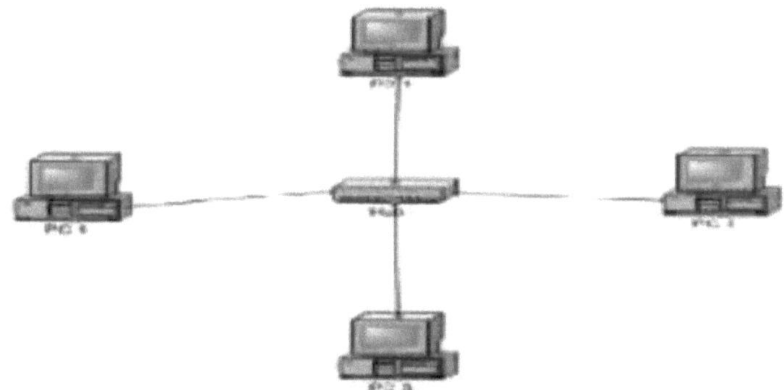

Fig.IV.3 : Star topology.

IV.3. CLASSIFICATION OF COMPUTER NETWORKS

The classification by extent of geographical coverage is often used, although not strictly.

They are classified according to their size or the distance between their nodes and their transmission modes. There are small networks (PAN), medium networks (LAN), large networks (MAN) and very large networks (RAN, WAN), even covering the whole world like the Internet.

IV.3.1. Personal Area Networks (PAN)

PAN, an acronym for Personal Area Network, refers to a restricted network of IT equipment usually used for personal purposes, interconnecting personal equipment such as GSM terminals, laptops, organisers, etc. for the same user over a distance of a few metres.

IV.3.2. Local area networks (LANs)

A local area *network*, often referred to by the acronym LAN, corresponds in size to an intra-company network. They are used to transport all the company's digital information. Generally speaking, the buildings to be wired extend over several hundred metres.

The speeds of these networks today range from a few megabits to several hundred megabits per second.

A network on a relatively small geographical scale, for example a computer room, a private home, a building or a company site.

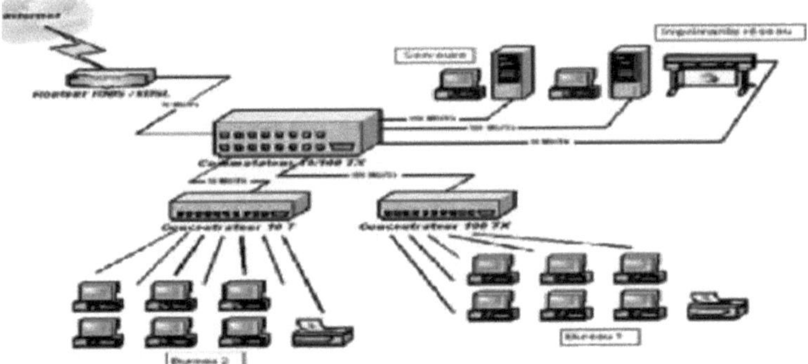

Fig.IV.4 : Local network

In the case of a corporate network, we also use the term LAN for corporate local area network.

Packet sniffers and frame analysers: o tcpdump
o Wireshark (formerly Ethereal)
o PRTG

Screen

In computer networks, a frame is a block of information carried across a physical medium (copper, optical fibre, etc.), and is located at level 2 of the OSI model.

The characteristic of a frame is that it is possible to recognise its beginning and end (thanks to a particular series of bits called a flag or preamble).

A frame consists of a header, the information to be transmitted, and a *trailer.* A packet (in the case of IP, for example) cannot transit directly over a network: it is encapsulated inside a frame.

IV.3.3. Metropolitan networks

A Metropolitan *Area Network* (MAN) is a network of computers usually used on campuses or in cities. The network generally uses fibre optics.

For example, a university or college might have a MAN that links together several local networks located in an area of 1 km2. Then, from the MANs, they could have several WANs linking them to other universities or to the Internet.

In the same way as a WAN, a MAN can be the *"backbone"* of a network.

Intranet.

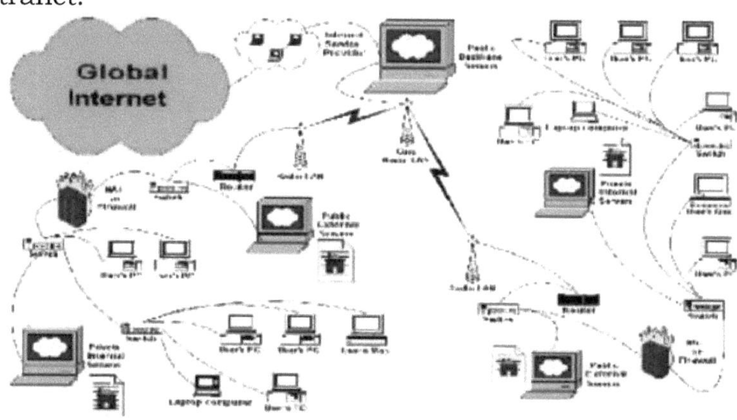

Fig.IV.5 : The metropolitan network

IV.3.4. Extended networks

A Wide Area *Network* (WAN) is a computer network covering a large geographical area, typically a country, a continent or even the entire planet. The largest WAN is the Internet.

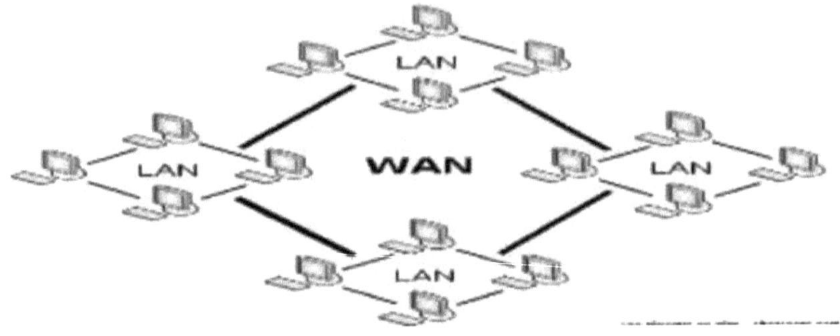

Fig.IV.6 : The extended network

IV.3.5. Other networks

a. **Storage Area Network (SAN)**

In computing, a storage *area* network (SAN) is a specialised network for pooling storage resources.

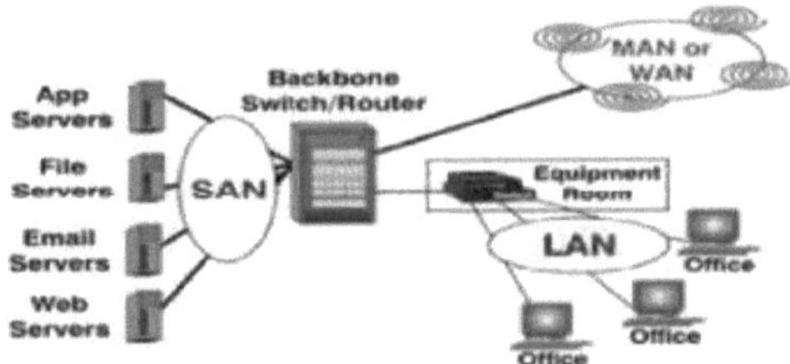

Fig.7 : The SAN network

b. Intranet

The intranet is a computer network used within a company or any other organisational entity using Internet communication techniques (IP, HTTP servers). In large companies, the intranet is subject to special governance because of its pervasiveness throughout the organisation. The main areas of corporate *intranet development* are :

S Accessibility of content and services; v' Integration of resources;

S Rationalisation of infrastructures.

IV.5. The OSI (Open Systems Interconnection) reference model

-* A model based on a principle enunciated by Julius Caesar: "Divide and conquer".

H) The basic principle is to describe networks in the form of a set of superimposed layers.

H) The study of the whole is reduced to that of its parts, and the whole becomes easier to manipulate.

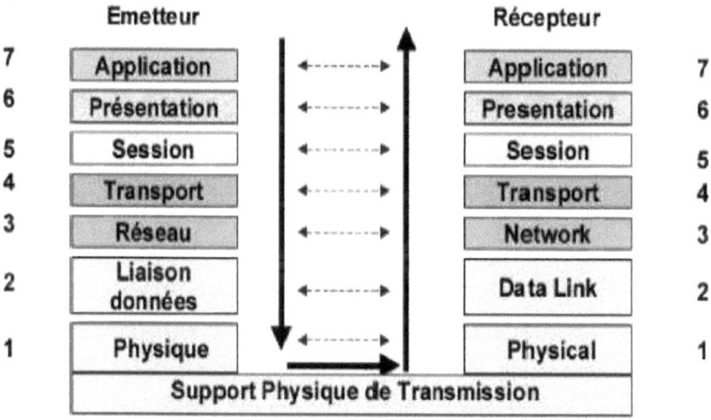

Fig.IV.8 : The OSI model

Level 1. The physical layer

Physical support + physical layer

ISO standard 10022 or ITU recommendation X.211 defines the service that must be provided.

It provides the mechanical, electrical and functional means for maintaining and deactivating the physical connections used to retransmit binary elements between link entities.

Transmission of bits on a communication circuit

The elements of the physical layer :

> Physical support

> Encoders, modulators

> Multiplexers, concentrators

The design of the physical layer can really be considered to be the domain of the electronics engineer.

Level 2. The data link layer

Uses the physical layer

Data link management

> Transmitter data in data frames,

> Transmission of frames in sequence,

> Recognition of frame boundaries sent by the physical layer

Error detection and recovery

> Traffic regulation,

> Error management,

Transmission procedure (HDLC, LLC, DSC, etc.)

ISO standard 8886 or ITU recommendation X.212 defines the service provided by layer 2.

Level 3. The network layer

It determines transport routes and handles message processing and transfer: manages IP and ICMP.

Level 4 Transport layer.

There are several classes of transport depending on the quality of the preceding layers. The more complete the lower layers, the less work the transport layer has to do, and vice versa. We deal with flow control, error recovery and packet reordering. We have TCP (INTERNET transport) which is an example, although it was developed independently of ISO standardisation.

Level 5 Session layer

We will see with TCP/IP that only 4 layers are seen instead of 7 in the model. In Session, we negotiate the establishment of the connection with the remote site, we open and close sessions with remote sites. Resynchronisation points are set (to restart in the event of a problem at a specific point).

Level 6 Presentation layer

It takes care of data formatting, a system language to harmonise the various services. In a way, they are the entry points to the operating system.

Level 7 Application layer

It manages the transfer of information between programs. All network applications, messaging, file transfer, etc.

Routing equipment only implements the first three layers. Only the source and destination computers implement all 7 layers.

IV.6. Safety

Security is an essential function of networks. Since you can't see your correspondent directly, you need to authenticate him or her. Since we don't know where the data is passing through, we need to encrypt it. Since we don't know if someone is going to modify the information sent, we need to check its integrity. We could add a long list of similar requests that need to be handled by the networks.

Broadly speaking, security can be divided into two parts: security at session opening and security during information transport. The techniques for achieving these two forms of security are extremely diverse, and new ones are being invented every day. In the same way, with each successful attack, hackers go one step further to bypass the defences. This game of chase is not likely to make the presentation of security mechanisms any easier.

The security of information transport is a primary concern in the field of networks. For many years, the security of a piece of equipment required complete isolation from the external environment, and no communication with an external machine was possible. This is still very often the case today.

Three main concepts have been defined:

Security functions, which are determined by actions that could compromise the security of an establishment.

Security mechanisms, which define the algorithms to be used.

Security services, which represent software and hardware that implement mechanisms to provide users with the security functions they require.

Five types of security service have been defined:

Confidentiality, to protect data from unauthorised attack.
Authentication, to ensure that the person logging on is actually the person whose name is given.
Integrity, which guarantees that the data received is exactly as issued by the authorised issuer.
Non-repudiation, which ensures that a message has been sent by a specified source and received by a specified receiver.
Access control, whose function is to prevent access to resources under defined conditions and by specified users.

IV.7. Intelligence in networks

Intelligence is a classic term in computing, which simply refers to the ability to communicate, reason and decide. Until the early 2000s, intelligence in networks was very low. The concepts of intelligent networks, which date from the early 1990s, introduce primary intelligence, whose role is to automatically adapt network components to user requests, but without reasoning and solely by following predefined rules.

Until recently, information was transmitted orally or in writing, mainly by telephone, telex and fax.

Today, the use of specialised networks enables all types of information carriers to be routed: sound, computer data, images, video, etc. We have entered the era of multimedia application communications, which represent a bridge between telecommunications and computing, two fields whose formal boundaries remain blurred.

The complexity of these networks and their applications is growing all the time, and it is essential to have the right support to control and manage these environments.

It is with this aim in mind that intelligence is entering networks in force. This chapter examines the elements capable of bringing this mastery to networks.

Several specific administration domains already use intelligent components, including the following:

S Configuration (configuration management) ;
S Security (security management) ;

- Fault management ;
- Performance audit (performance management) ;
- Accounting (accounting management).

Artificial intelligence means putting yourself in the place of a human being to carry out a task.

The expression "intelligent networks" refers to another category of networks, which are networks that can adapt quite simply to the introduction of a new service.

These networks are completely different from those that incorporate intelligent agents.

The network architectures developed to date can only support simple services, requiring a single application, such as e-mail services, file transfer, transaction processing, etc.

The network architectures developed to date can only support simple services, requiring a single application, such as e-mail services, file transfer, transaction processing, etc.

It is possible to combine several applications to create a new service using the architecture set up in the application layer. For example, an EDI (electronic data interchange) document can be transported in an electronic message.

The complexity of managing and controlling network equipment increases enormously when you move beyond the network and integrate applications.

Users want to have a global view of the service they are requesting, from its operation to its cost, including security and quality of service issues.

The simplest thing for users would be to be able to define exactly what they want from the network. The role of the intelligent network is precisely to be able to adapt to user demand.

Intelligent networks were one of the major projects of the 1990s for the world of telecommunications. Although most operators are using intelligent network concepts, the huge upheaval expected, which should have permeated all the telecoms world's network products, has not taken place.

This relative failure stems from too rapid an evolution in telecommunications and the adoption of the IP world for future telecommunications networks.

The concept of the intelligent network has been taken up in part in the application world of Internet networks in an attempt to adapt the Internet's transport mode to applications.

Protocols such as SOAP (Simple Object Access Protocol) can be seen as computer languages aimed at creating an intelligent Internet network.

The natural evolution of intelligent networks is towards autonomous networks.

These are capable of configuring themselves and taking the place of conventional systems, which often rely on a control centre or particularly complex distributed algorithms.

IV.8. Internet

Intelligent networks were one of the major projects of the 1990s for the world of telecommunications. Although most operators are using intelligent network concepts, the huge upheaval expected, which should have permeated all network products in the telecoms world, has not taken place. This relative failure stems from too rapid an evolution in telecommunications and the adoption of the IP world for future telecommunications networks.

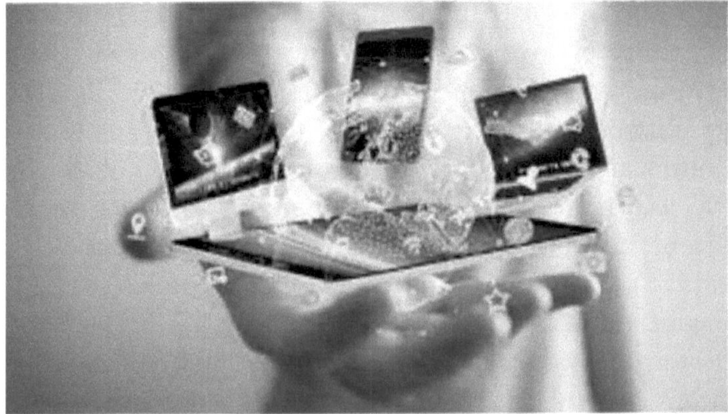

The concept of the intelligent network has been taken up in part in the application world of Internet networks in an attempt to adapt the Internet's transport mode to

applications.
Protocols such as SOAP (Simple Object Access Protocol) can be seen as computer languages aimed at creating an intelligent Internet network.
The natural evolution of intelligent networks is towards autonomous networks. These are capable of configuring themselves and taking the place of conventional systems, which often rely on a control centre or particularly complex distributed algorithms.
For the media and the general public, the World Wide Web (WWW, or W_3) and the Internet are one and the same. The WWW is one of the most widely used services on the Internet. It is made up of sites.
What's more, companies are tempted to create an Internet network, Intranet, and set up Web servers.

The three basic services :
File transfer: the Internet is used as a vast library distributed across the planet. Viewed as a library of files of all types, and in particular software, made available to everyone, wherever they may be, thanks to the ftp (File Transfer Protocol) file transfer service. This service is used in academic and research environments.
Connecting to a remote computer: connecting to remote computers is widely used in the scientific world. The rlogin (remote login) or telnet commands have been around since the beginning of the network and enable work to be carried

out in distributed mode, i.e. it is possible to use the resources available on the remote computer, such as computing power and databases.

Email, electronic mail: The electronic mail service enables messages to be exchanged with millions of people around the world, 1 IP address of the machine managing the mail service.

The Internet was originally a communications infrastructure network. Its development has led to an explosion of associated tools (servers, browsers, specialised software, mobile terminals, applications, etc.) and generated new social practices.

In so doing, it is simultaneously giving rise to a major economic space and a mental space, as well as a large-scale ideological production about the network and its uses. It is this ensemble, between the production of new artefacts that encode information in binary and the ideology that accompanies this new domain, that we call the 'digital'.

In this area, we have gone from adjective to noun, indicating the pre-eminence of the discourse around employee technologies over the technical form of the devices concerned. Whereas our lives and our relationship with the world are based on analogue channels (the five senses), remote transmission, reproduction and interaction have become encoded mainly in binary.

The strength of the term "digital" is that it avoids the term "calculation". We need to calculate in order to encode in binary the information gathered either from individuals (texts, images, videos, etc.) or directly from sensors increasingly associated with our environment, both personal (geolocation) and urban (the "intelligent city" and its host of information captured in public places: pollution, presence, travel times, etc.).

Computation is also needed to make this information available again to the senses of the individuals involved in digital communications. This twofold computational phenomenon means that many blocking or derivation points can be put in place. The digital knowledge factory is an invisible world, to which only the designers hold the keys. This is the case with DRM (Digital Rights Management systems), which require the decoding tool to have a digital key, the absence of which renders a digital document unusable. The same applies to the interception of messages, and their diversion to computing powers that will extract profiles, relationships and signals that will enable individuals to be better targeted according to commercial interests (advertising and commercial profiling) or strategic interests (mass surveillance, the existence and methods of which Edward Snowden has made tangible).

At the heart of this calculation are algorithms, mathematical processes, but also the inscription in computer code of human reasoning, with all the biases and presuppositions that this entails. We can thus speak of a "politics of algorithms" to describe everything that disappears from the eyes of the players in interaction *via* digital networks.

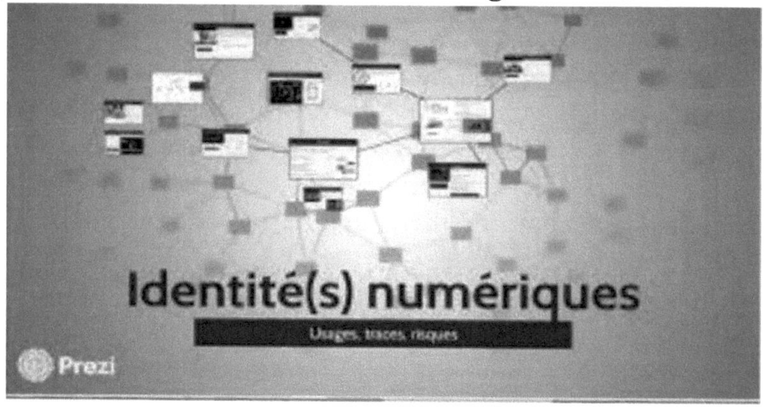

CHAPTER V

MODELLING THE DIGITAL LIBRARY PROBLEM

In this chapter, we focus on the actual behaviour of users of digital libraries, their expectations and their perceptions, defending the following idea: the user and his characteristics must be taken into account when designing a digital library. In this sense, we are defending a user-centred approach as opposed to the techno-centred approach that is all too often seen.

V.1 User-centred library

<< If we build it, they will come ", Such seems to be the leitmotiv of many designers of digital libraries and political decision-makers: " if we build it, they will come ". The pronoun "they" refers to the users, while "we" refers to the designers.

We need to better understand users' needs and behaviour if we are to create a library that is relevant, useful and usable for those same users.

V .2. False beliefs

There are beliefs among designers and/or users that we would describe as false because they are erroneous. These beliefs concern new technologies, and the Internet in particular, and some of them are largely sustained by the prevailing media discourse.

False belief 1: <<users are getting better and better at handling and mastering new technologies". We must not confuse the ease with which users handle peripherals and/or certain technical objects (such as remote controls or *joysticks*) with the ease with which they handle the information flows conveyed by these peripherals or technical objects. We can therefore distinguish between two types of procedural knowledge that need to be acquired and developed: procedural knowledge linked to the handling of peripherals and procedural knowledge linked to the process. However, there is a great risk of believing that users "understand everything that goes on behind the screen"

because they manipulate the keyboard and mouse without fear and do not hesitate to "launch themselves onto the web". In addition, there are two important points to note: firstly, not all users of the digital library like computers; secondly, from a purely manipulative point of view, using computers can be difficult for some people.

False belief 2: "all young people love computers and the Internet". Some young users have a distrust, sometimes a fear or even an anxiety about computers. In fact, it's wrong to think that just because a user is young, they like computers! What's more, in recent years a growing number of studies have focused on this computer-related anxiety, which can persist in adults who categorically refuse to use new technologies.

False belief 3: "quantity = quality of information". When users are asked to search for information on the Internet or in any other digital documentary environment, it is not uncommon for some to come back with "packets" of information or lists of printouts of Internet pages and/or documentary references. These users (students) seem to be engaged in a quantitative strategy to the detriment of a qualitative strategy, the latter requiring them to read, understand and assess the relevance of the information or references selected.

False belief 4: "I can do without the expert and be autonomous". The ease of access to computers and their content leads some users to believe that the expert (teacher, librarian, librarian, etc.) is of no use to them.

False belief 5: "tool = process". Searching for information and/or documents is above all an intellectual process. For some users, however, there is confusion between the information-seeking process and the tools that can be used to search for information. For example, when we ask young users (students) if they know how to search for information on the Internet, many answer "yes, because I know how to use Google".

However, many of the steps involved in searching for

information and/or documents (e.g. choosing key words, selecting sources of information) can be carried out independently of the presence of IT tools. While being aware that these beliefs are erroneous is a necessity, it is not enough to ensure that users' actual behaviour is correctly understood. Their expectations and real needs must be identified before our digital library is designed.

V .3. User expectations

After interviewing a number of students from the Faculty of Science, we found that the three main expectations of users of our digital library are as follows:

S The content must be easily accessible and not require any particular technical or documentation skills;

S A digital library must offer the same services as a traditional library, such as displaying the latest new acquisitions, managing the borrowing of books, etc. ;

J A digital library must be designed in such a way that the user finds his or her "marks", such as obtaining help from employees.

V .3.1. Functionality

J Users should be able to filter and/or organise and/or classify the results offered by the digital library's internal search engine;

J The content, or at least part of the content, should be downloadable;

J A personal history should always be available so that every Users can store their searches and related results so that they can be retrieved for future use;

J Systems should enable and support collaborative searching for information (for example, by sharing "baskets" between several users).

V .3.2. At the interface and usability level

J The format in which results are presented (references and/or documents) should be identical and consistent;

J Search results should fit on a single page;

V .3.3. Content

- a digital library should contain all formats (videos, images, sound, etc.);
- a digital library should make it easy to move on to other digital libraries.

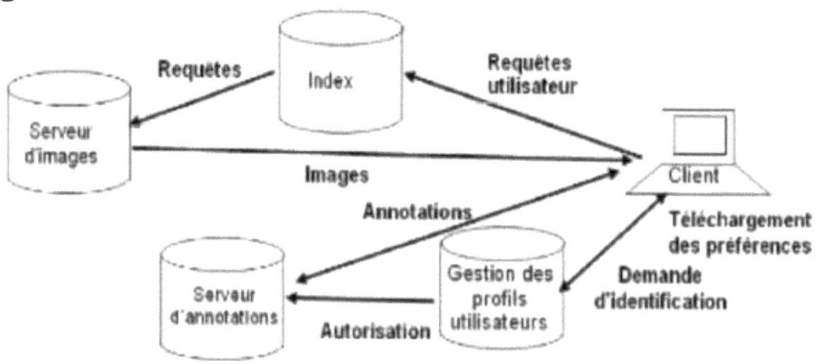

Fig.V.1. classic scheme for managing a digital library with* the *database

V.4 Specifications

We want to create a virtual library. Two types of user will be able to access the site. The first is the Internet user looking for a book (the customer), who wishes to consult a book from their Internet browser. The second type is the site administrator, who manages the online download page from their web browser.

We have drawn up a list of requirements for each of these types of user.

> . Customer requirements

> Customers can access the online library using a browser that complies with the HTML 4 standard or higher.

> Customers can search for and select books anonymously, but they must identify themselves or fill in a registration form as soon as they validate the list of articles chosen, in order to download. With this in mind, data managed during the session (virtual basket or shopping cart) ensures that the items selected by the customer are memorised before the download is confirmed. However, as soon as the customer

confirms the download, all the information required for delivery is recorded in the server database.

> Customers search for an item by selecting a theme or entering the name (or part of the name) of a work in a search field in the catalogue. The search result is displayed in the form of a list of brief information (reference, author, etc.), and the customer can view the record for each item by simply clicking on the reference of the book required. The record for a book contains all the information about the book (reference, title, author, description, cover photo). If they wish, customers can add the item to their virtual basket by clicking on a special hypertext link in the item file.

> The customer can change the desired quantity of each item selected, and possibly delete some of them from the virtual basket screen. However, they can no longer modify their download once it has been validated.

> After logging in again, the customer follows the status of their download, which can take two values: *Waiting*, for orders that are valid but waiting to be connected, and *Delivered*, for orders that have been sent to the customer.

+ Administrator requirements

> The administrator manages the site from their web browser. > The administrator must identify himself to access his online administration space, and a single login/password pair is configured for this purpose.

> The administrator can delete customer accounts and modify their information.

> The administrator adds, deletes or modifies items in the catalogue.

V.5. Information storage

a. Design of the user identification system

On arrival at the virtual library, the user is identified anonymously by PHP's integrated session management system. This anonymous session identifier follows the user throughout their visit to the site. If the user is a customer, his session initially enables him to remember the items added to his virtual basket (see table 2 below).

When the order is validated, the customer declares their identity by entering their e-mail address and password, or creates a customer account if they do not already have one. Once the customer account has been validated, the customer's e-mail ($_SESSION ['email']) and status ($_SESSION ['status'], equal to customer in this case) are added to the virtual basket data in the session (see table V.1).

It should be noted that, during this stage, the user's order information and contact details are saved in the server database, so that they can be retrieved on a future visit. If the user is an administrator, his session only remembers his e-mail address and status when he enters the identification form. By remembering their admin status, they can access all the pages in the administrator area, without having to log in when moving from one page to another.

Table V.1: Session variables used to identify a user

Variables from session dedicated to identification	Description	Examples
$_SESSION	User e-mail address	mushila@unikin.cd
['email']	(customer or Director)	
$_SESSION ['status']	User status, which is set to client or admin depending on the user profile.	customer

b. Designing the virtual shopping basket

As we said earlier, the information relating to the items selected by the user is stored in session variables. We use an array variable ($list I]) to store all the information in the virtual basket list.

This first array itself contains as many array variables as

there are items to be retained (Ix] represents the identifier of each item). Each item array stores four different items of information (Iy]=0: reference, Iy]=1: quantity,).
The resulting structure is therefore a two-dimensional array ($listeIx]Iy]). To understand how this $liste variable works, we'll illustrate its use with a concrete example of an order for three items (VB, Telematics and Database).
In this example, it is possible to retrieve the quantity information from the database item using the variable $listeI2]I1] (which is equal to 1 in the example).

$list Ix]Iy]	Iy]=IO] : reference	Iy]=I1]: quantity
[x]=[0] : articleO	VB	2
[x]=[1] : article 1	Telematics	3
[x]=[2] : article2	Database	1

c. Database design and production

We call the application's database the Digital Management Library (Biblionumerique), which is made up of five tables according to the specifications below.
Structure of the Biblionumerique database

> Articles table - groups together the fields characterising the various parameters of the articles in the library (reference, author, description, etc.).

> Topics table - defines the names of the topics under which the articles are classified.

> Download table - groups together the fields characterising an order (date, customer ID, download status, etc.).

> Lists table - groups together the fields characterising each item ordered (item reference, quantity ordered, etc.).

> Customer table - groups together the fields characterising each customer (surname, first name, address, e-mail address, password, etc.).

V .6. Challenges and prospects for the virtual library

It should be noted that the Virtual Library has benefited from a *clear and coherent vision,* both in terms of its objectives and its operating plan, since its conception phase, and that it has been able to rely on a *stable and high-performance technical platform.* A number of challenges remain:

S Speed up the pace of digitisation (volume of digitised educational documents),

S Manage updates to already classified documents,

S Resolve the problem of broken links for documents located on other servers,

S More control over the display of results when the user uses the Virtual Library's search engine (classification criteria, etc.).

S Raising the profile of the Virtual Education Library among users

S Ensure the involvement of partners (sources of documents),

S Take into account the new technologies related to content publication that have emerged over the last two years (RSS feeds, Podcasts, Blogs, P2P networks, etc.),

S Taking advantage of new document management technologies, particularly intelligent content management systems (ICMS)

CHAPTER VI

DIGITAL TRANSFORMATION AT ISG-KINSHASA

While the use of Customer Relationship Management (CRM) tools seems to be a must, the deployment and implementation of these technological solutions is not as straightforward as it might seem. The close integration with business processes, as well as the strategic role of the technological solution, call for very specific project management.

VI .1. Principle

www.piloter.org

Open source, e-commerce management and Social CRM, which are in full development, need to be given due consideration in order to put the process of measuring and improving customer value into action as it should be.

You can't buy a CRM solution off the shelf. Customer Relationship Management is a strategic project. In all cases, the impact on the way the organisation operates is sufficiently significant for us not to venture to consider this project lightly. Before embarking on the project to implement the solution, whatever its scale, it is essential to know what we are talking about. Comments by defining and summarising the principles of the software.

To manage a business project, complex by nature, it's not

enough to know the methods and tools of the trade. The slightly experienced project manager knows full well that he or she will be able to resolve the difficulties inherent in the project by starting to create the right conditions for mutual trust between the men and women in the team, as well as with the other stakeholders. In short, it's all about using a good dose of common sense. But you still need to know how to put it into action.

The information technologies that support information systems are constantly evolving and shaping the internal structures of these systems. Innovation, which has been particularly dynamic over the last two decades, is continually redefining their uses. To better grasp the strategic opportunities offered by information technologies, it is highly advisable to look at their principles.

Presentation of our digital transformation project at the Institut Supérieur de Gestion in Kinshasa

Teacher dashboard (Student management)

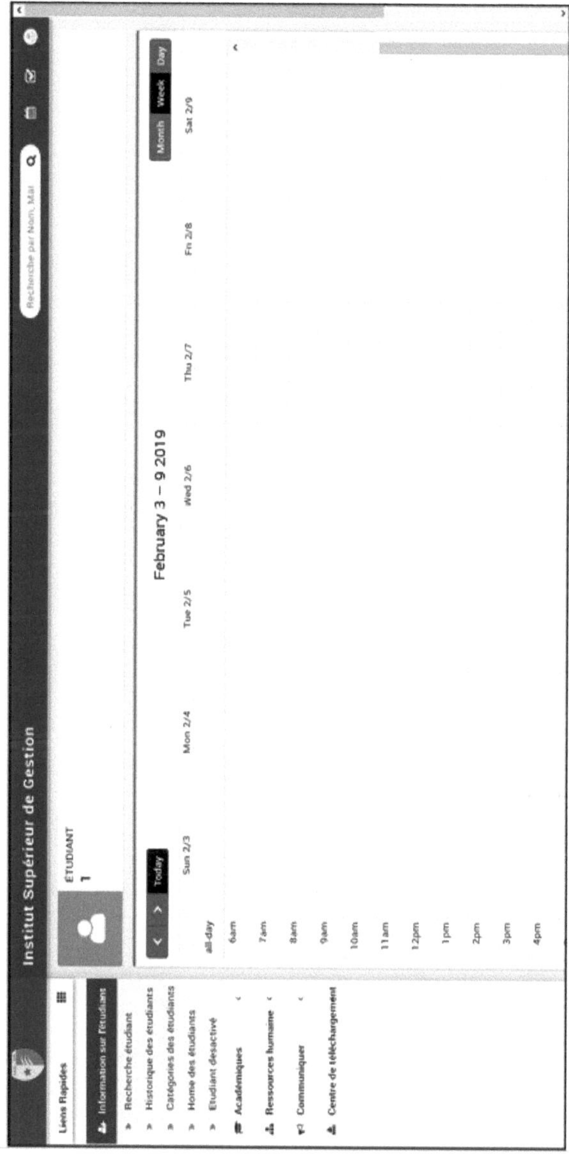

Academic section for Teachers

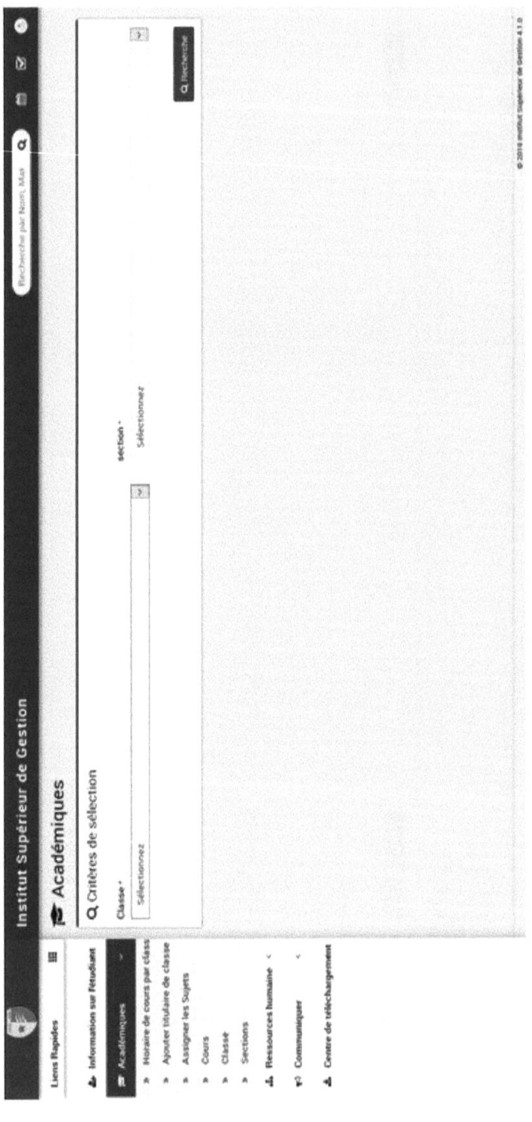

View the list of agents and their telephone numbers

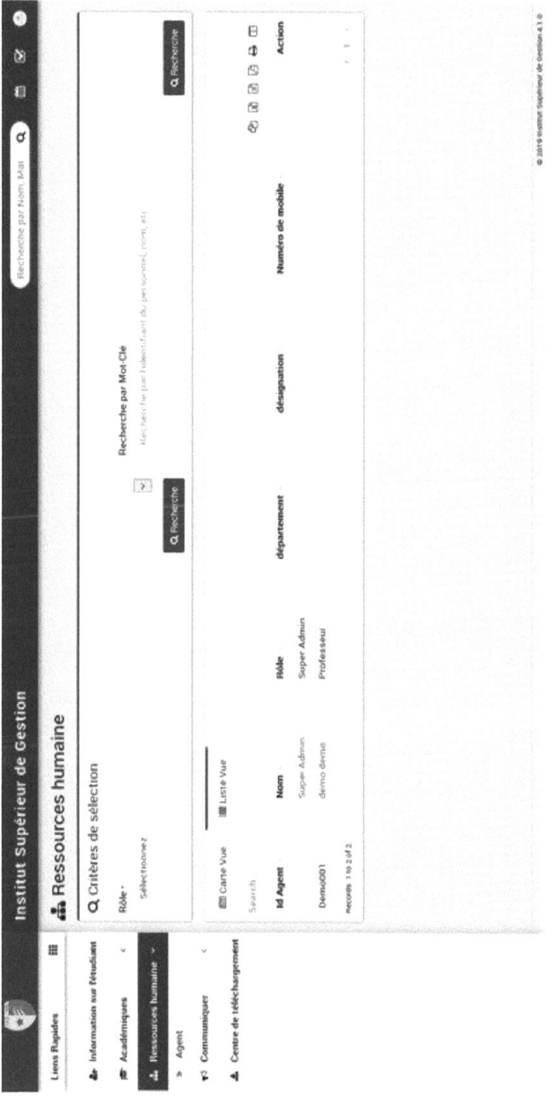

Possibility of sending messages using the digital valve

Ability to add files for download (e.g. Syllabi)

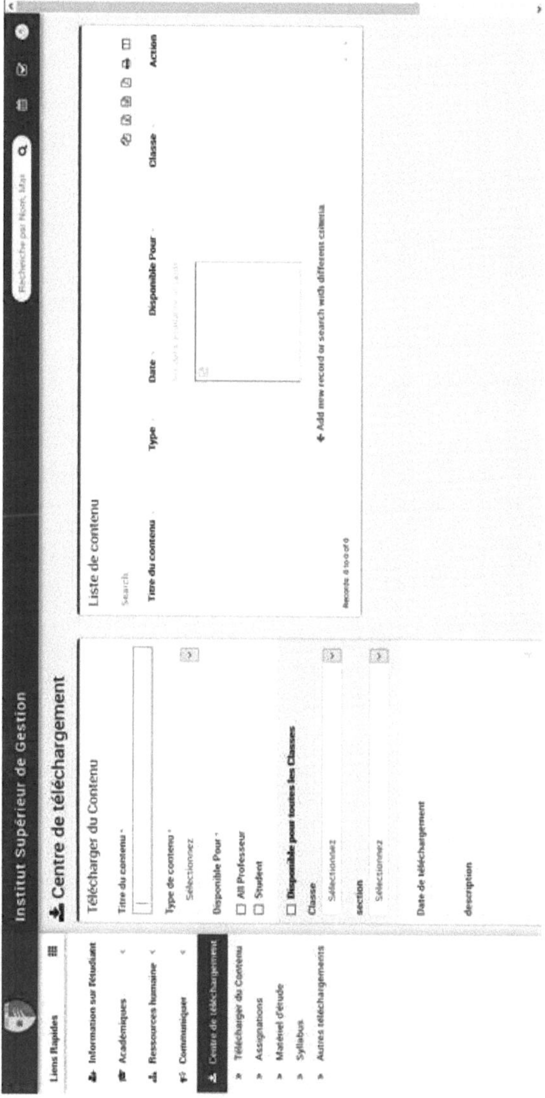

Student dashboard

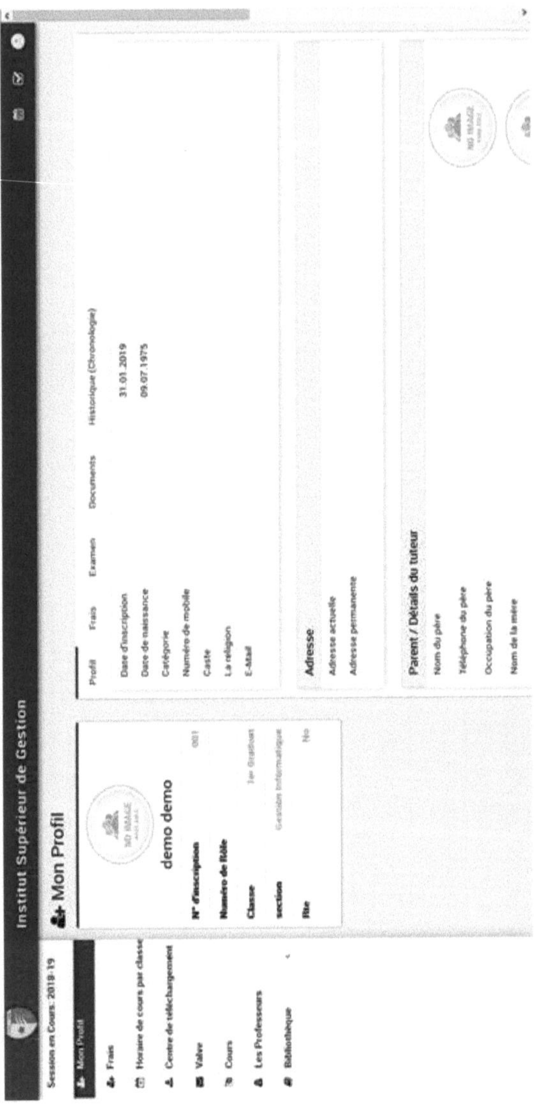

Ability to add academic documents directly

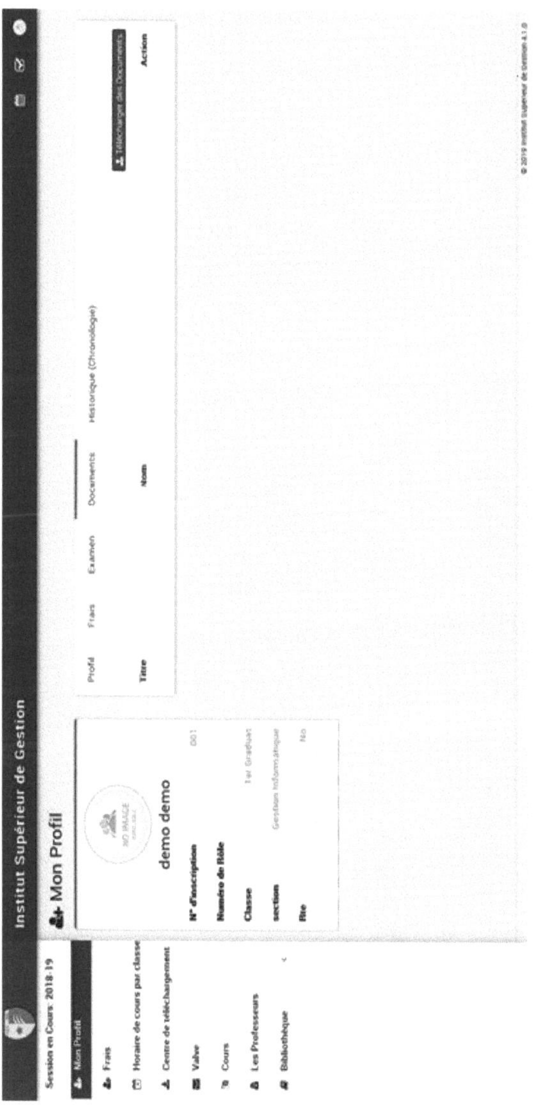

View your course timetable

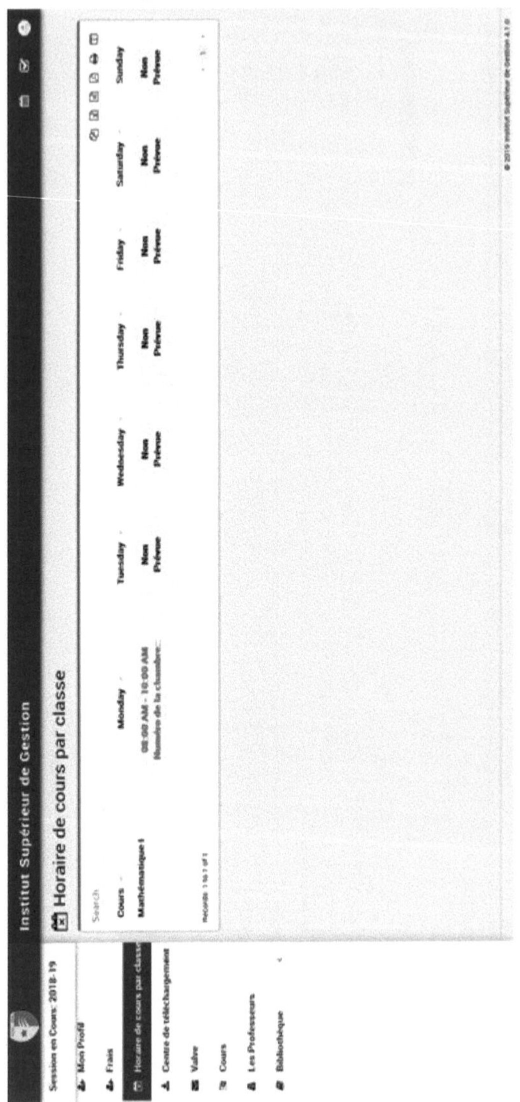

View the list of courses

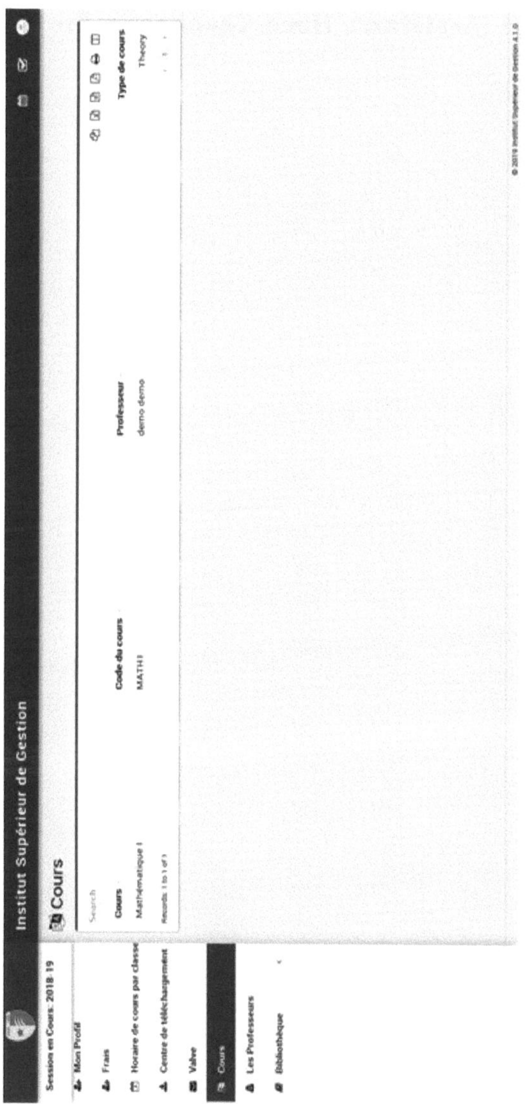

You can view the list of teachers and their respective grades (Assistant, Head Teacher or Professor).

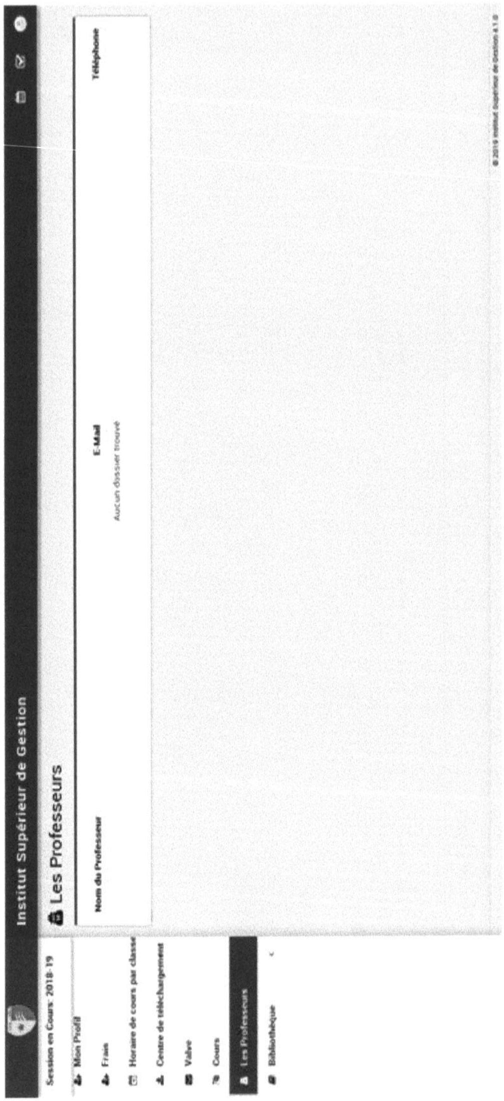

View books available in the library with prices and quantities

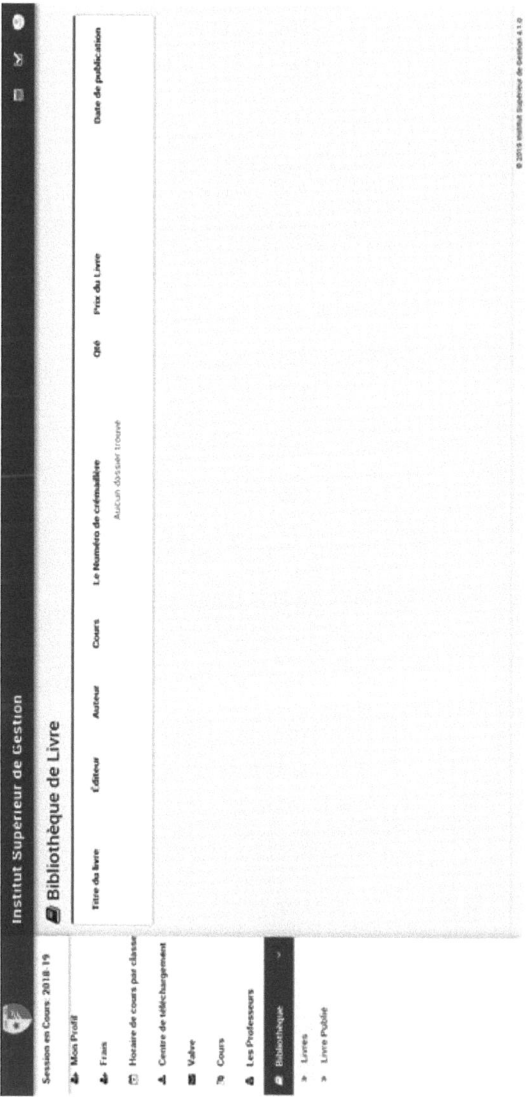

Parent dashboard with the option of viewing children's profiles

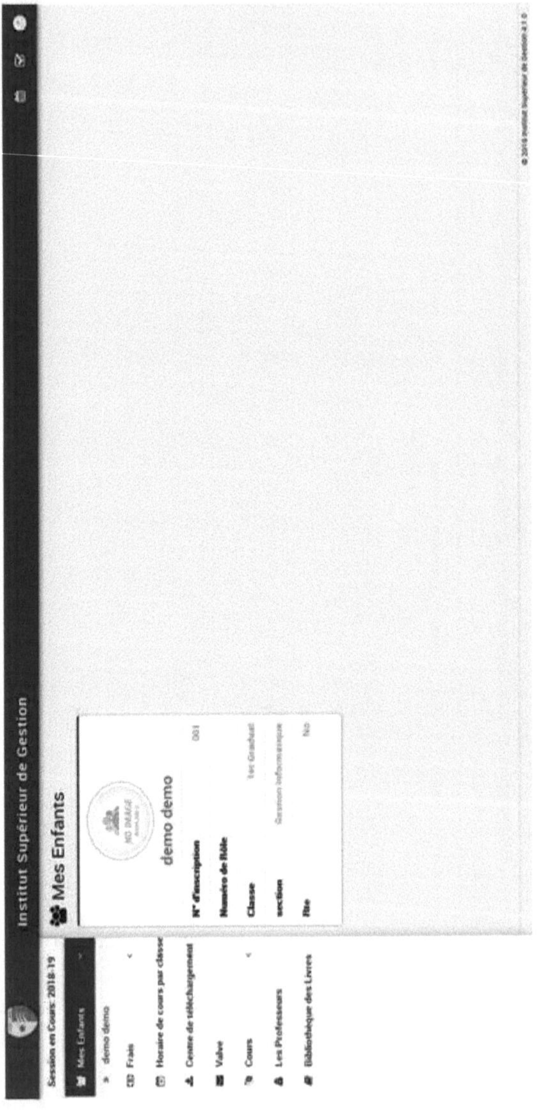

Possibility of tracking the costs of each Student

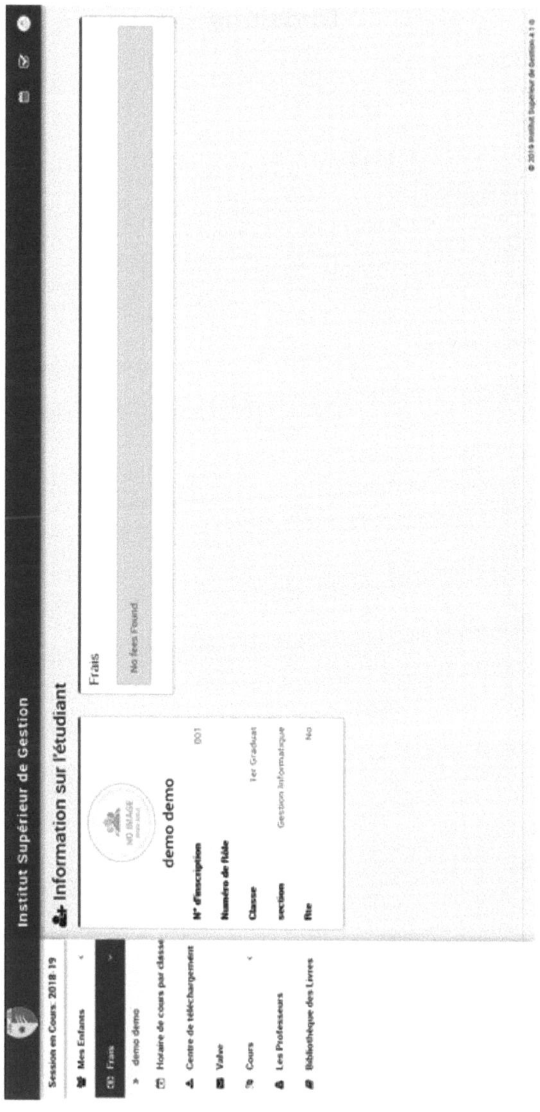

View the course timetable for each Promotions and Divisions

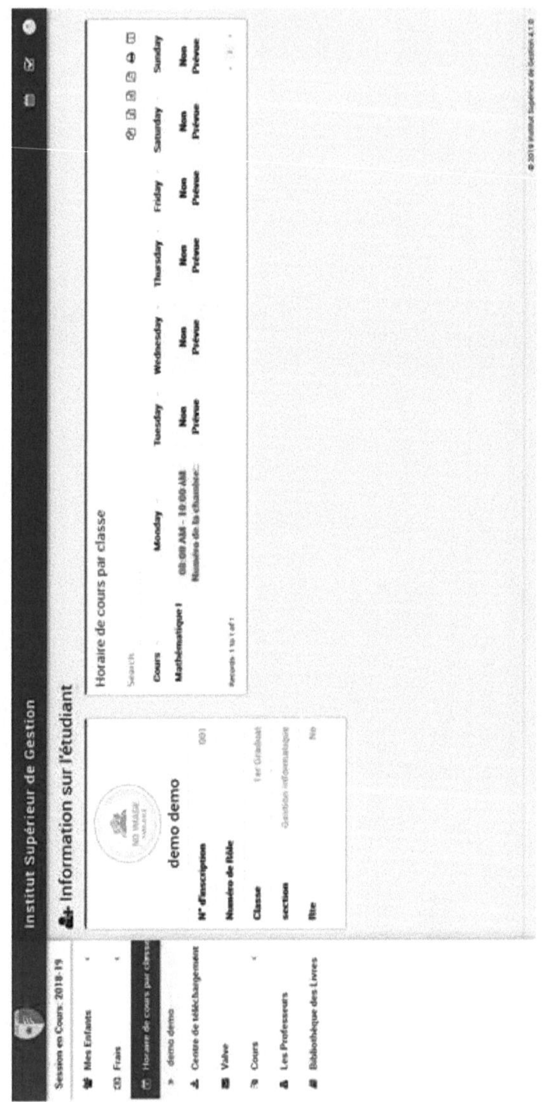

View download list

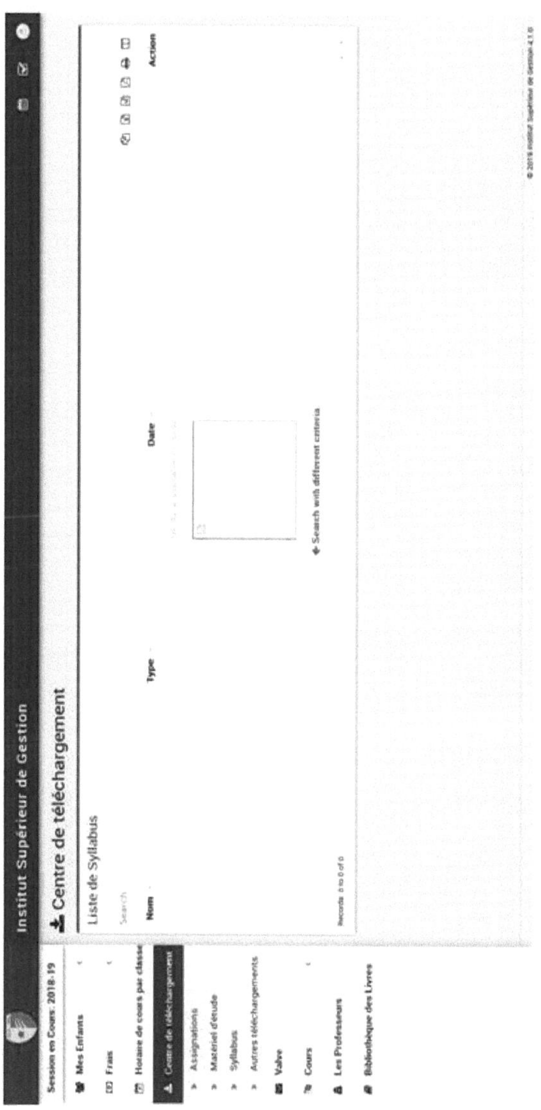

View press releases directly from your account

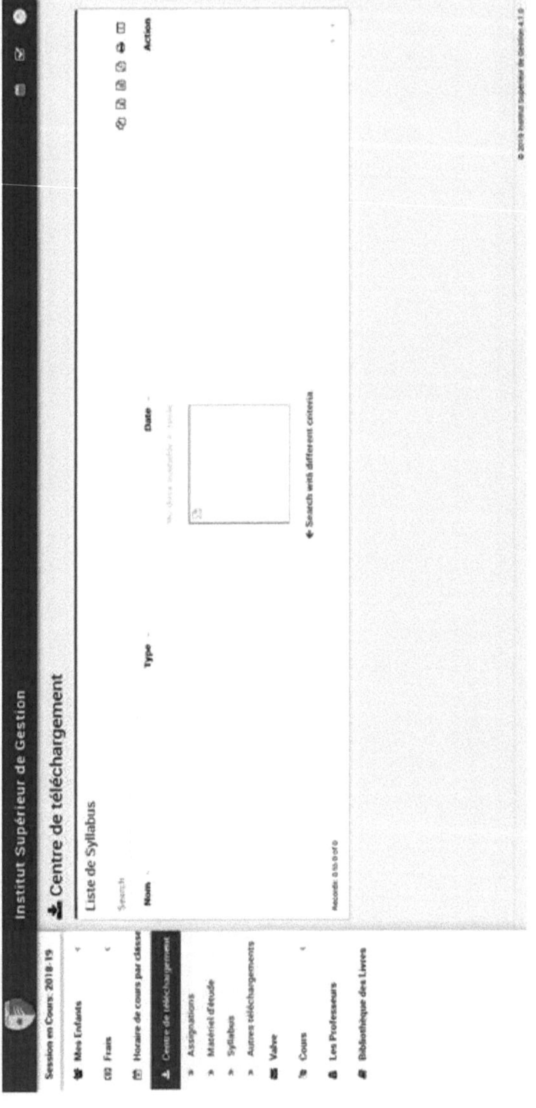

Accounting dashboard

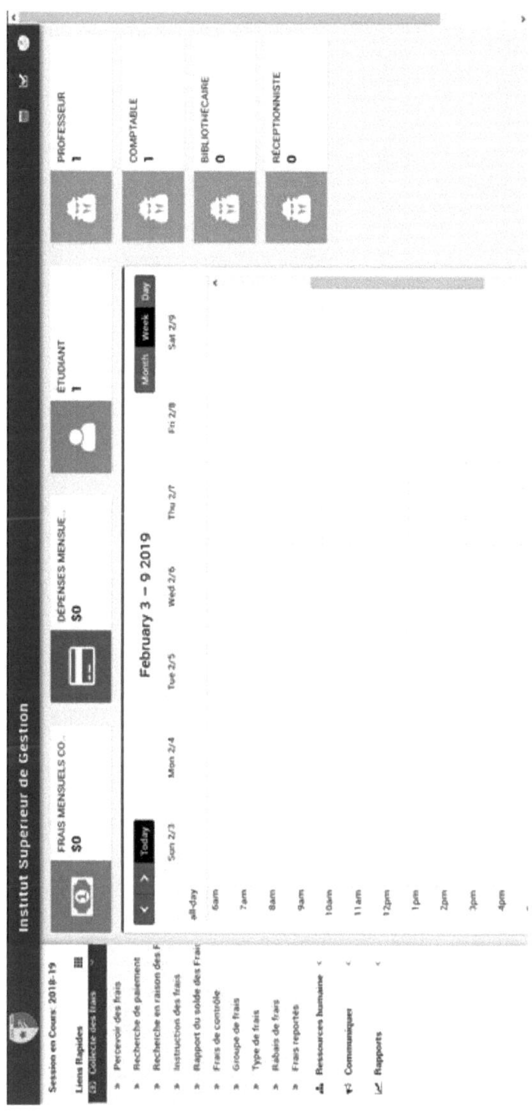

Search for payments

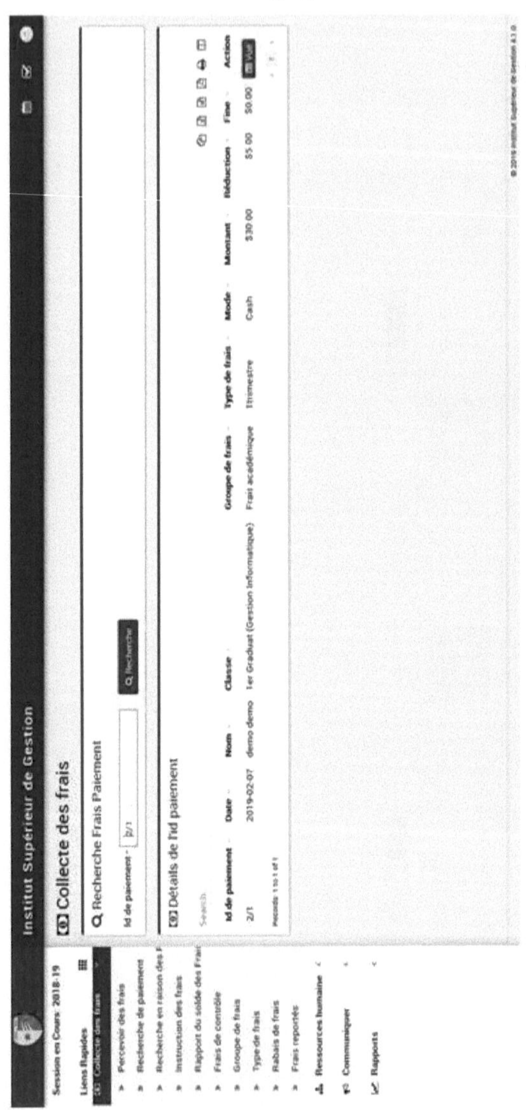

View each student's payment history

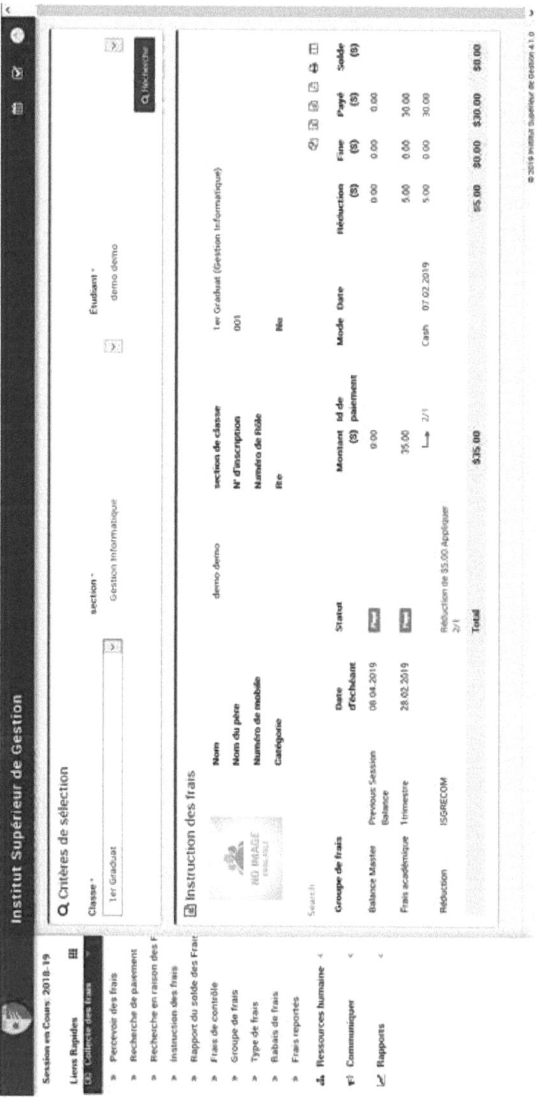

You can view the fee balances for each Student

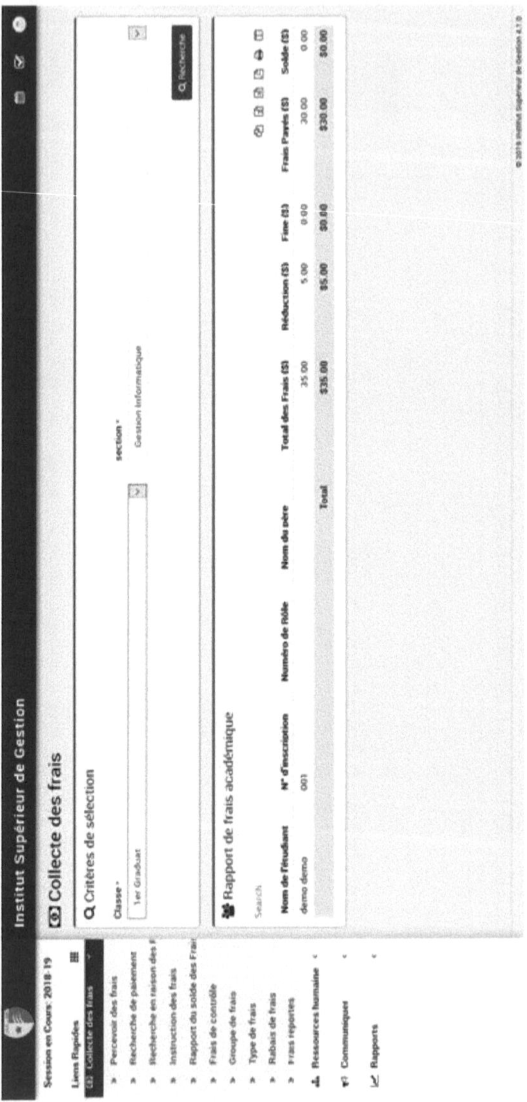

Ability to add and assign payments

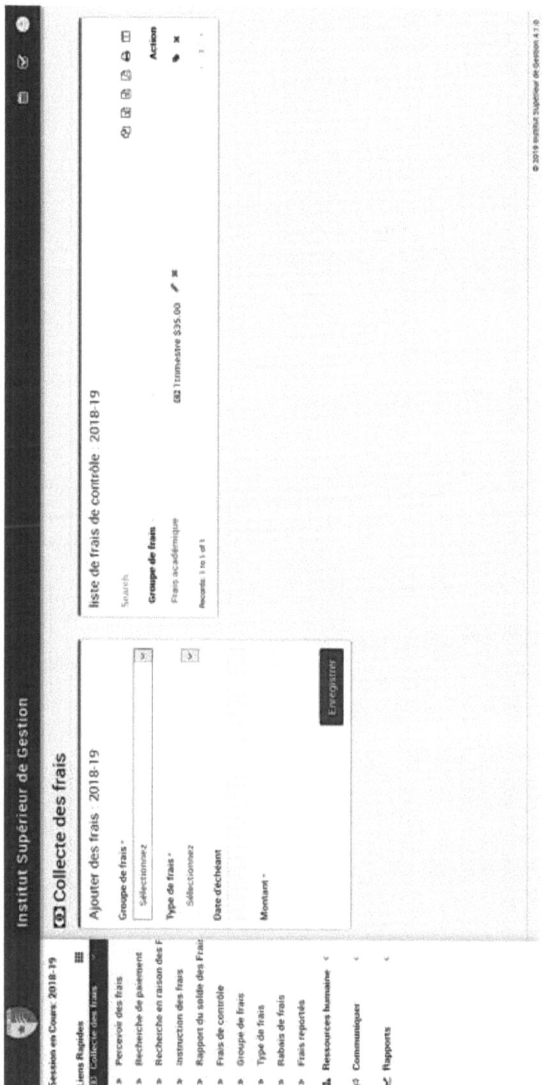

Possibility of grouping costs

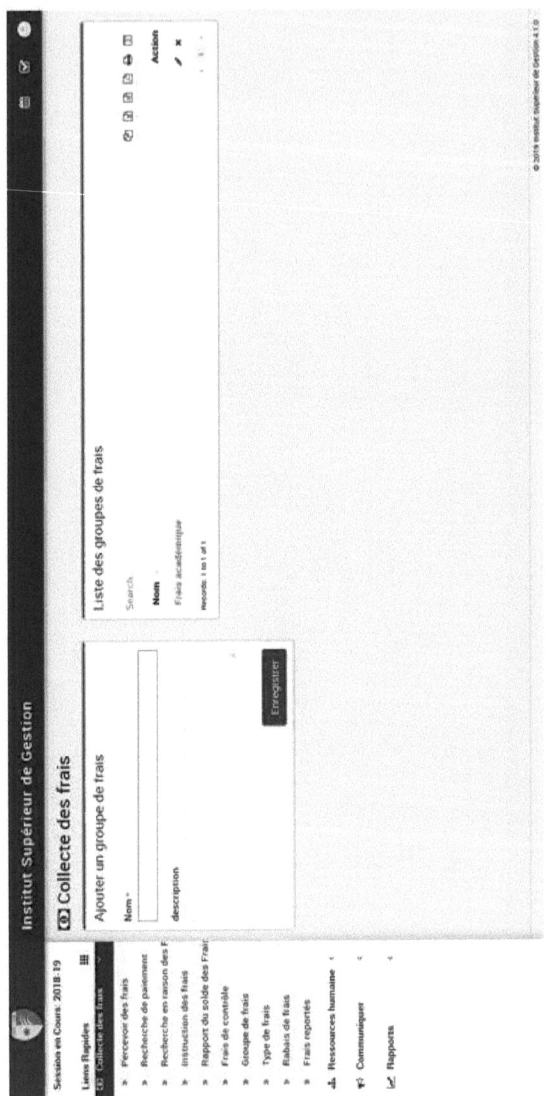

Each fee can be denominated (e.g. 1st quarter)

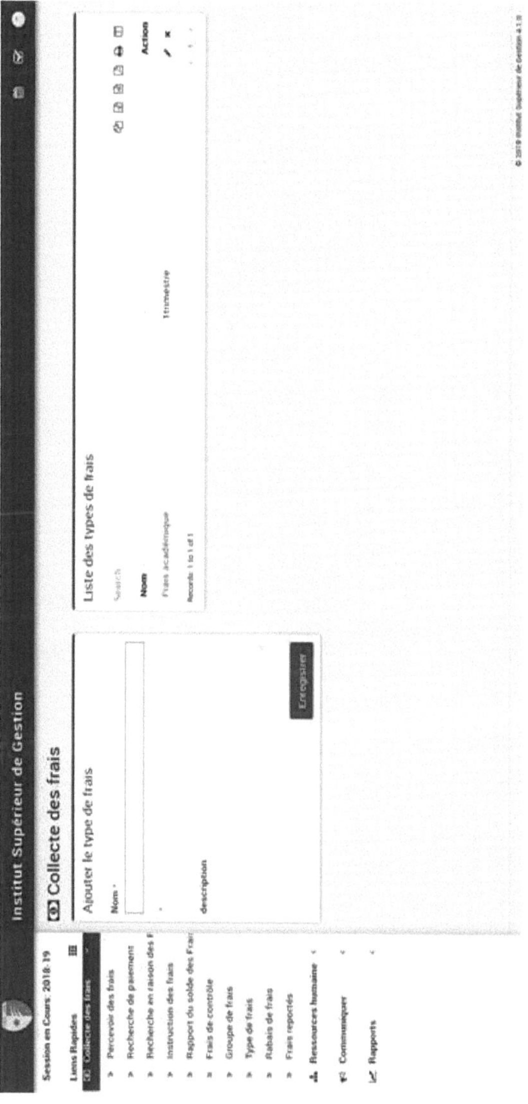

Ability to create discounts (e.g. for registered mail)

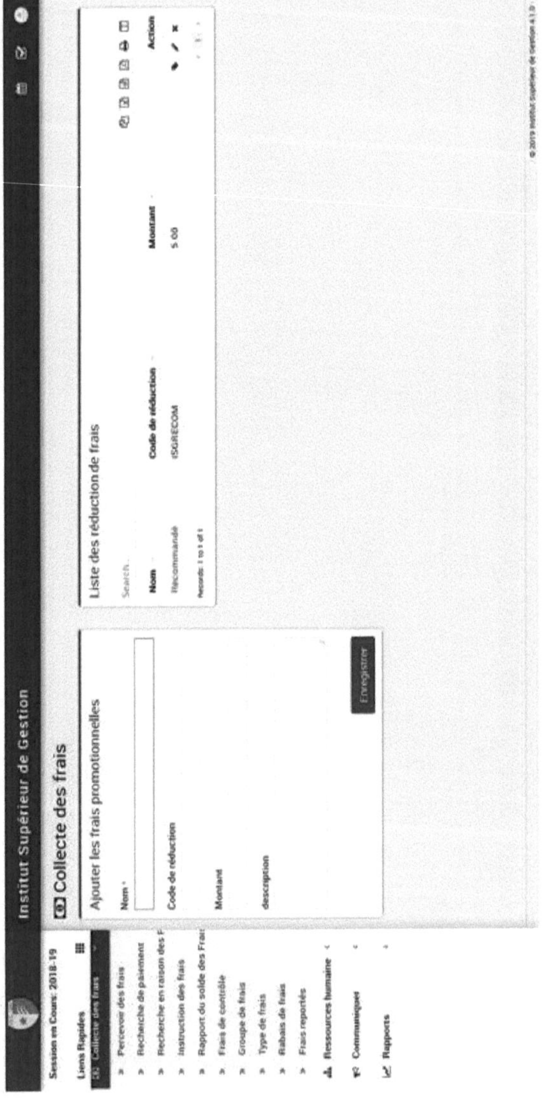

Possibility of collecting balances from the previous year

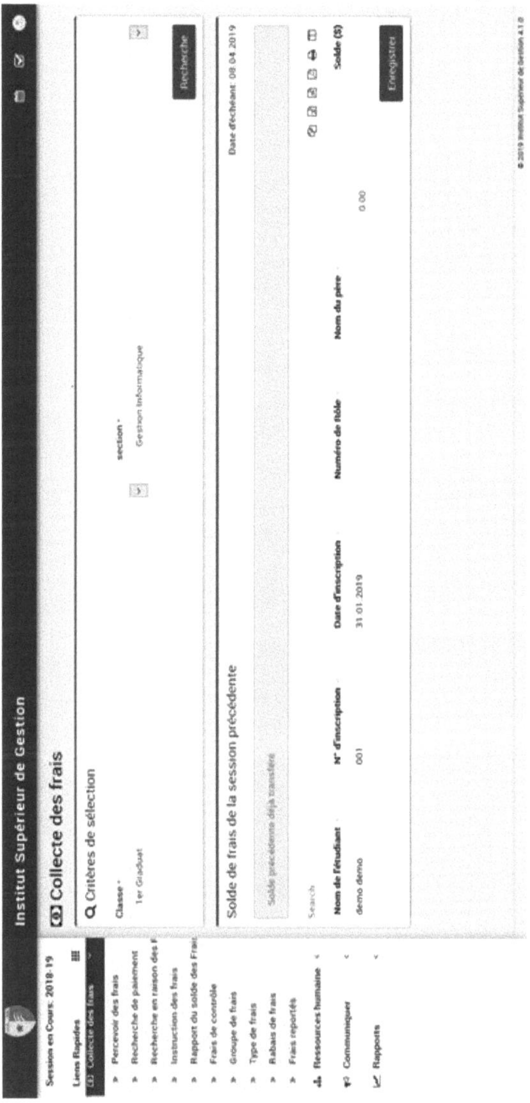

View the list of agents

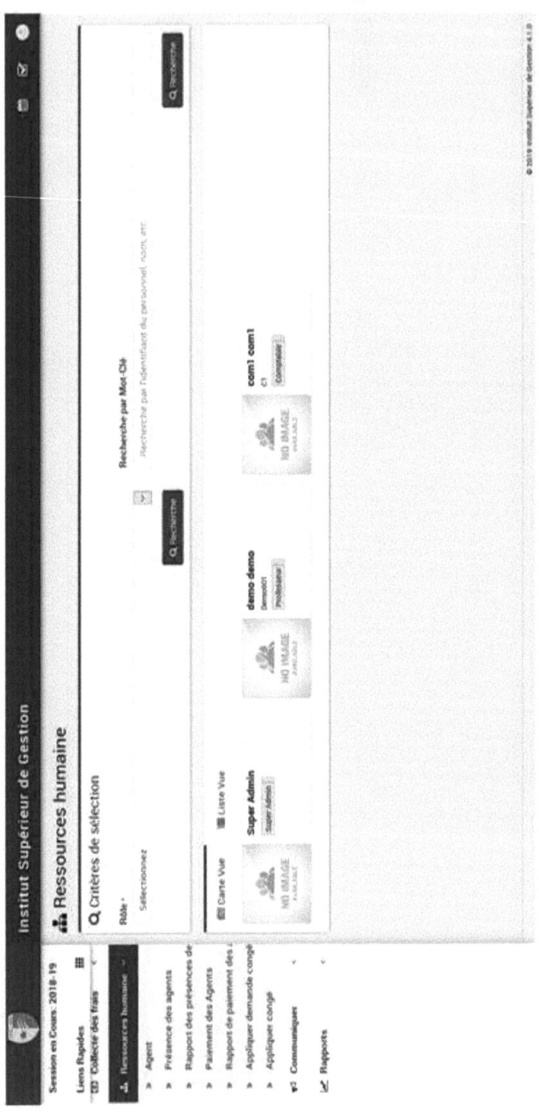

View the attendance report

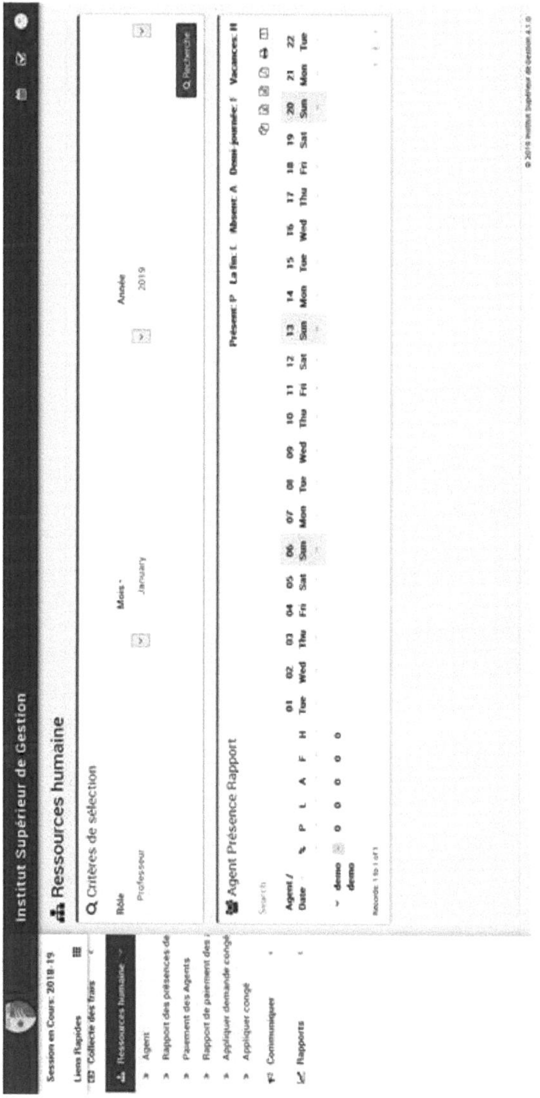

Ability to calculate and pay staff salaries

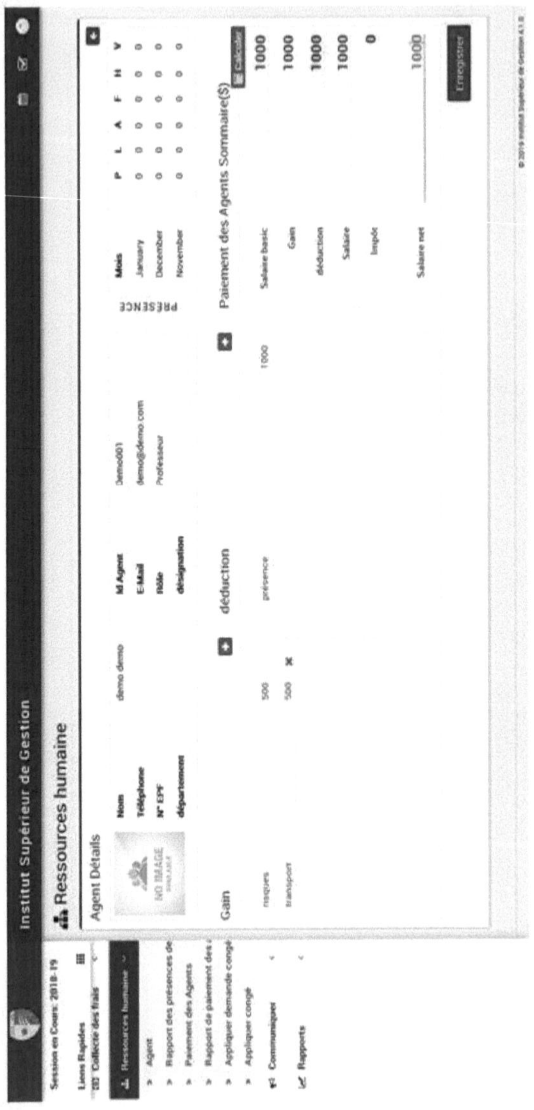

View the payment report

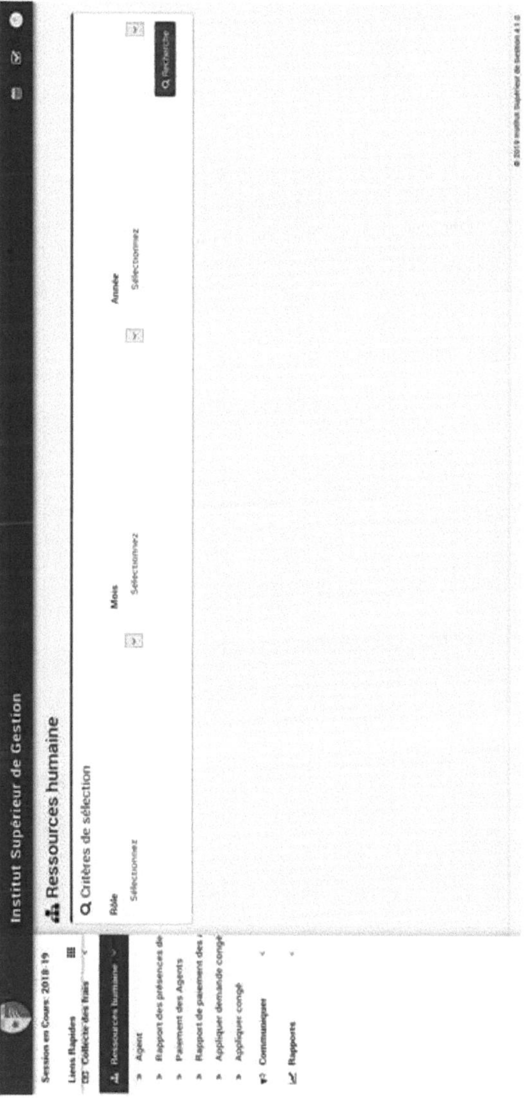

Possibility of communicating with all Teachers

View connection reports

Institut Supérieur de Gestion

Session en Cours: 2018-19

Liens Rapides

- Collecte des frais
- Ressources humaine
- Communiquer
- Rapports
  - Instruction des frais
  - Rapport du solde des Frais
  - Rapport de transaction
  - Rapport de paiement des
  - Rapport des présences de
  - utilisateur log

Rapports

utilisateur log

Tous les utilisateurs | Agent | Etudiants | Parent

Search

Utilisateurs	Rôle	Adresse	Heure de connexion	Utilisateur
com1@demo.com	Comptable	127.0.0.1	07.02.2019 13:58:01	Firefox 64.0, Windows 10
parent1	Parent	127.0.0.1	07.02.2019 13:47:37	Firefox 64.0, Windows 10
std1	Student	127.0.0.1	07.02.2019 13:30:14	Firefox 64.0, Windows 10
demo@demo.com	Professeur	127.0.0.1	07.02.2019 12:56:43	Firefox 64.0, Windows 10
festa@isgkin.nga	Super Admin	127.0.0.1	07.02.2019 12:51:04	Chrome 71.0.3578.98, Windows 10
festa@isgkin.nga	Super Admin	127.0.0.1	06.02.2019 16:02:33	Chrome 71.0.3578.98, Windows 10
festa@isgkin.nga	Super Admin	127.0.0.1	06.02.2019 15:59:23	Chrome 71.0.3578.98, Windows 10
festa@isgkin.nga	Festa	127.0.0.1	06.02.2019 15:55:10	Chrome 71.0.3578.98, Windows 10
festa@isgkin.nga	Festa	127.0.0.1	06.02.2019 15:47:34	Chrome 71.0.3578.98, Windows 10
festa@isgkin.nga	Super Admin	127.0.0.1	06.02.2019 14:17:40	Chrome 71.0.3578.98, Windows 10
festa@isgkin.nga	Super Admin	127.0.0.1	05.02.2019 15:12:57	Chrome 71.0.3578.98, Windows 10
festa@isgkin.nga	Super Admin	127.0.0.1	02.02.2019 14:25:11	Chrome 71.0.3578.98, Windows 10
festa@isgkin.nga	Super Admin	127.0.0.1	01.02.2019 17:01:32	Chrome 71.0.3578.98, Windows 10
std1	Student	127.0.0.1	01.02.2019 12:12:06	Chrome 71.0.3578.98, Windows 10
festa@isgkin.nga	Super Admin	127.0.0.1	01.02.2019 12:10:01	Chrome 71.0.3578.98, Windows 10
festa@isgkin.nga	Super Admin	127.0.0.1	31.01.2019 22:42:28	Chrome 71.0.3578.98, Windows 10
festa@isgkin.nga	Super Admin	127.0.0.1	31.01.2019 13:52:57	Chrome 71.0.3578.98, Windows 10
festa@isgkin.nga	Super Admin	127.0.0.1	30.01.2019 16:48:20	Chrome 71.0.3578.98, Windows 10

GENERAL CONCLUSION

We have now come to the end of our Master's thesis in Digital Communication, which focused on the following theme: **Digital Transformation: a lever for optimal management of a company in the face of globalisation.**

Our study was carried out at the Institut Superieur de Gestion de Kinshasa (ISG-Kin), which has existed since 2003 in the Democratic Republic of Congo, in the city of Kinshasa.

The main objective of this work is to enable the Institut Superieur de Gestion de Kinshasa to meet the needs of its clients, in the face of the demands imposed on us by the revolution in new technologies and the implementation of the LMD (Licence-Maitrise-Doctorat) system.

In addition to the above, increasing sales and standing out from the competition by integrating digital transformation is an innovative solution.

In this work, we confirm that, faced with the upheavals in today's environment (fierce competition, technological change, robotisation, globalisation, etc.), no-one can deny that *"digital transformation"* has become an unavoidable and indisputable factor in optimising the management and integral development of any company concerned with preserving its survival.

The Institut Superieur de Gestion de Kinshasa is currently evolving in an unprecedented competitive environment, surrounded by almost ten (10) other higher education and university institutions, whereas five (5) years ago it was almost alone in the area.

To make it easier for our readers to understand, and to reach a rational conclusion, we have considered the Institut Superieur de Gestion to be a product in its mature phase.

This phase is characterised by the following elements:

S The maturity phase is when product sales begin to stabilise after rapid growth.

S So the product has found its place and sales have peaked.

Similarly, today the Institut Superieur de Gestion de Kinshasa has found its place and the number of students

currently exceeds 19,000, proof of its rapidly growing stability. What's more, some of our competitors are using the same strategies as ISG-Kinshasa, in particular that of cutting costs by reducing tuition fees, which consequently reduces the effectiveness of the strategy itself.
As far as the management process for academic fees is concerned, payment receipts are still compiled manually, and recorded in notebooks that are supposed to contain the details of all the students who come to pay, even though we are a Higher Management Institution.
As a result, it is difficult to easily find information about the student who paid the fee, because it is not known in which document (registration book) this information is found and some students have several codes for themselves.
This situation jeopardises the management of this major process of managing academic fees, given that it is the main process that enables ISG-KIN to generate revenue.
Another case is that of the main library of the Institut Superieur de Gestion in Kinshasa, which has a capacity of 30 people, whereas the estimated number of students is currently more than 18,000. If we assume that 60 students can consult this library every day, it will take another 300 days for all the students to have access to it, which will be equivalent to 10 months, i.e. even longer than the period planned for an entire academic year.
This leads us to confirm our hypotheses on the integration of digital transformation, which we present in the following stages:
S Digitising the library and automating the library helpdesk with chatbots
S Link your data to your processes
S Move each course online
S Monitoring the student lifecycle, from admission to graduation
S Numerise all payment processes
This Master's thesis is structured into six chapters, which

have enabled us to gain an overall understanding of the concepts behind digital transformation, in order to make the Institut Superieur de Gestion de Kinshasa a new product.

To achieve this, user satisfaction, usage and impact on the organisation, both individually and collectively, are criteria that need to be taken into account. However, we must not overlook the difficulties involved in determining and measuring the indicators needed to produce dashboards. Understanding management information systems therefore requires a cross-disciplinary and multi-disciplinary approach (information systems have technical, strategic, organisational, behavioural and sociological dimensions, etc.).

It is undoubtedly also necessary to include in this Master's thesis the fact that the information system is not a fixed system; it changes, transforms itself by assimilating technological mutations and adapting to the strategy and structural choices of organisations. It accompanies these changes, not only following them but also influencing them. In this way, the information system is both a witness to, and a player in, corporate change.

This is no longer just a time for cutting costs and mastering the teaching programmes organised at ISG-KIN, but rather a time for innovation, which is now an essential condition for the survival and development of many companies. However, if innovation is to be transformed into a convincing success on the market, it must be conditioned by the implementation of a management and organisational structure conducive to its development.

Finally, we would like to inform you that this work is not perfect, and may contain errors, given that it is written by an imperfect person.

We are convinced that our work will also serve as a benchmark for all researchers who would like to work on a similar theme.

BIBLIOGRAPHY

I. WORK

- **Azan,W. et Beldi,A.,** 2011, " *De la cybernetique a la theorie de la human agency : vers un management des SI cent sur les utilisateurs* ", Management & Avenir, n°39, pp.192-212
- ALBANO Charles (1974) - *Transactional analysis on the job* - Amacom.
- ALLEN Thomas (1977) - *Managing the Flow of Technology: Technology Transfer and the Dissemination of Technological Information Within the R&D Organization* - The MIT Press.
- ALTER Norbert (2002) - L'innovation ordinaire - PUF.
- ALTSHULLER (1988) - *Creativity as an exact science (pocket mathematical library)* - CRC Press.
- ARGYRIS Chris and SCHON Donald (1978) - *Organizational learning: a theory of action perspective* - Addison-Wesley.
- ASSELIN Caroline & THAI Antoine (2007) - *La creativite ne sinvente pas, elle se manage!* - Les editions Demos. -
- **Beaufils,B., Brandouy,O., Ma,L., et Mathieu,P.,** 2009, "*Simuler pour comprendre : un eclairage sur les dynamiques de marches financiers a I'aide des systemes multiagents", systemes d'Information et Management*, vol. 14, n°4, pp.5170
- **Bezes C.,** 2012, "*La congruence perque des magasins et du site Internet: effets sur le choix du canal d'achat - le cas de la Fnac*", Vie & sciences d'entreprise, n°190, pp.46-70
- BADOT Olivier (1998) - Theorie de l'entreprise agile - L'Harmattan.
- BASSO Olivier (2004) - *L'intrapreneuriat* - Economica.
- BAUMOL William (2002) - *The free-market innovation Machine: Analyzing the growth miracle of capitalism* - Princeton University Press.
- BELANGER Laurent, MERCIER Jean (2006) - *Auteurs et textes classiques de la theorie des organisations* - Presses Universite Laval.
- BETZ Frederick (2003) - *Managing technological*

innovation: Competitive advantage from change - John Wiley & Sons.

- BLANCO Sylvie & LE LOARNE Severine (2009) - *Innovation management* - 2009
- BOY Jacques, DUDEK Christian, KUSCHEL Sabine and CHAVET Rudolf (2003) - *Management de projet* - De Boeck.
- BOOZ Edwin, ALLEN James & HAMILTON Carl (1982) - *New product management for the 1980s* - BAH, New York.
- BURNS Tom and STALKER George (1963) - *The management of innovation* - Oxford University Press.
- BRAUDEL Fernand (1985) - *The Dynamics of Capitalism* - Flammarion.
- BRUNET Thierry et al (2005) - *Management of organisations* - Breal
- **Caseau,Y.**, 2008, Urbanisation, SOA et BPM - *Le point de vue d'un DSI,* Dunod.
- **Chanegrih,T.,** 2012, *"Les outils de controle de gestion : entre stabilite et changement",* Management & Avenir, vol. 8, n°58, pp.95-115
- CATMULL Edwin (2008) - The Pixar Touch: The Making of a Company - Knopf.
- CHANDLER Alfred Dupont (1962) - *Strategies et structures de l'entreprise* - Editions D'organisation.
- CHRISTENSEN Clayton Michael (1997) - *Innovator's dilemma: When New Technologies Cause Great Firms to Fail* - Harvard Business Press.
- CHESBROUGH Henry William, VANHAVERBEKE Wim & WEST Joel (2006) - *Open innovation: researching a new paradigm* - Oxford University Press
- CARRIER Camille (1997) - *De la creativite d intrapreneurship* - PUQ.
- COSTER Michel (2009) - Entrepreneuriat - Pearson Education.
- CRUTCHFIELD Krech (1962) - *Individual in society A textbook of social psychology* - McGraw-Hill Book Company.
- **Deltour,F.,** 2012, *"TIC et innovation organisationnelle",*

Systeme d'Information et Management, vol. 17, n°2

- **Dinet,J.,** 2008, *Usages, usagers et competences informationnelles au xxie siecle,* Hermes.
- DELMOND Marie-Helene, PETIT Yves & GAUTIER Jean-Michel (2008) - *Management des systemes d'information* - Dunod.
- DYSON James (2005) - *The spirit of design* -Sw-Telemaque Editions.
- **Eynaud,P.,** 2010, *"Analyse comparative des strategies Internet de deux associations",* systeme d'Information et Management, vol. 15, n°1, pp.69-95
- EMERY Frederick Edmund (1969) - *System Thinking* - Penguin Books.
- GAREL Gilles (2003) - *Le management par projet* - La decouverte.
- GELINIER Octave (1968) - *Participative management by objectives* - People and techniques.
- GETZ Isaac (2003) - *Your ideas change everything!* - Editions d'Organisation.
- GIRARD Bernard (2006) - *Une Revolution du Management : le modele Google* - M21 Editions.
- HAMEL Gary (2007) - *The Future of Management* - Harvard Business Press.
- HALL Edward Twitchell (2008) - *The hidden dimension* - Seuil.
- HERRMANN Ned (1990) - The Creative Brain - Ned Herrmann Group.
- HUGUET Pascal & MONTEIL Jean-Marc (2001) - *The social regulation of classroom performances: A theoretical outline* - Social Psychology of Education.
- JOSEPHSON Matthew (1959) - Edison: A Biography - Wiley.
- JOLIVET Francois (2003) - *Manager l'entreprise par projets : Les metaregles du management par projet* - Management et Societe (EMS).
- KHANDWALLA Pradip (1976) - *The design of organizations*

- Harcourt Brace.
MACGREGOR Douglas (1960) - *The human side of enterprise* - McGraw-Hill.
MAILLAT Denis (1993)- *Innovation networks and environments*
innovateurs: un pari pour le développement regional - Neuchatel, EDES.
MALSEED Mark & VISE David (2005) - *The Google Story* - Thomas Arnold Publishing.
MARCH Gardner James & SIMON Herbert (1965) - Les organisations - Dunod.
MAYO George Elton (1933) - *The Human Problems of an Industrial Civilisation* - The Macmillan Company.
MINTZBERG Henri (1982) - *Structure and Dynamics of Organisations* - Editions d'Organisation (new version 1988).
MORITZ Michael (1984) - *The little kingdom: The private story of Apple computer* - William Morrow & Co.
NELSON Richard R. WINTER and Sidney G. (1982) - *An Evolutionary Theory of Economic Change* - Belknap Press of Harvard University Press.
NONAKA Ikujiro & TAKEUCHI Hirotaka (1995) - *The KnowledgeCreating Company: How Japanese Companies Create the Dynamics of Innovation* - Oxford University Press.
Lee D. (1992) - *Job Challenge, Work Effort, and Job Performance of Young Engineers: A Causal* Analysis - Engineering Management.
PIAGET Jean (1986) - *Le Structuralisme N°1311* - Presses Universitaires De France, collection Que Sais-Je.
PLANE Jean-Michel (2003) - *Theorie des organisations* - Dunod, 2nd edition.
PONS Francois-Marie & De RAMECOURT Marjolaine (2001) - *L'innovation a tous les etages : Comment associer les salaries a une demarche d'innovation* - Editions d'Organisation.
PORTER Michael (1985)- *Competitive Advantage: Creating and Sustaining Superior Performance* - Simon & Schuster Ltd.
RICARDO David (1817) - *Principles of political economy and taxation* - Electronic version.

SAADOUN Melissa (2000) - *Information technology and management* - Hermes Science Publications.

SAINSAULIEU Renaud (1977) - *L'identite au travail* - Presses de Sciences Po.

SAUTERON Francois (2009) - *La chute de l'empire Kodak* - L'Harmattan.

SENGE Peter (1991) - *The fifth discipline* - First.

SCHUMPETER Joseph (1912) - *Theory of economic revolution: Research on profit, credit, interest and the business cycle* - Electronic version with an introduction by Francois Perroux.

SCOTT & MITCHELL (1976) - *Organization of social activities* - Prentice-Hall.

SCULLEY John (1988) - *De Pepsi d Apple* - Grasset.

SMITH Adam (1776) - *An Inquiry into the Nature and Causes of the Wealth of Nations* - Electronic version.

STRASSER Christopher & POISTER Theodore (1982) - *Organizations must innovate to survive* - Pennsylvania State University, Great Valley.

TAYLOR Frederick Wilson (1911) - *The principles of scientific management* - Electronic version.

TWISS Brian (1992) - *Managing Technological Innovation* - Pitman (4th edition).

TERNINKO John, ZUSMAN Alla & ZLOTIN Boris (1998) - *Systematic innovation: an introduction to TRIZ* - St. Lucia Press.

TYLOR Edward Burnett (1876) - *Primitive civilisation* - Reinwald, French translation

VON HIPPEL Eric (1988) - *The source of innovation* - Oxford University Press

ZARIFIAN Philippe (2005) - *Skills and Strategies* Editions Liaisons.

II. Course Notes

1. NIKIANA MAZAMBA C., 2021, *Theorie des organisations et Management,* L1 Management, ISG-Kinshasa, Inedit, page 56

2. Gilbert ATASA, 2022, *Notes de Cours de NTIC, L1 Management,* UNIKIN, Inedit.

3. MAGUIRAGA, 2021, Cours de Cybercriminalite et Reseaux Informatiques, L1 Polytechnique, UNIKIN, Inedit.
4. MANSHIMBA KAPINGA J., 2022, Macroeconomie, L2 Toutes les Filieres, ISG-KIN, Inedit.

III. Theses and dissertations

FOREST Joëlle (1999) - *L'Economie de la conception au coeur du processus d'innovation* - These de Doctorat en Economie de la production, Universite Lumiere Lyon II, Faculte de Sciences Economiques et de Gestion.

GRANGE Louis-Alexandre (2008) - *Factors in stimulating creativity and the effectiveness of a cross-creativity process between two companies* - Master of Research in Economics and Innovation Management.

BOLDRINI Jean-Claude (2005) - *L'accompagnement des projets d'innovation : Le suivi de l'introduction de la methode TRIZ dans des entreprises de petite taille* - These de Doctorat en Droit et Sciences Sociales, Universite de Nantes, Faculte des Sciences Economiques et de Gestion.

ROMON Francois (2003) - *Le management de l'innovation, essai de modelisation dans une perspective systemique* - Doctoral thesis at the Ecole Centrale de Paris, Discipline: Management.

IV. Scientific articles

ALTER N. (1993) - *Innovation et organisation : deux legitimites en concurrence* - Revue francaise de sociologie.

AMABILE, T. M. & GRYSKIEWICZ S. (1987) - *Creativity in the R&D laboratory: How Environment and Personality Impact Innovation* - Handbook for Creative and Innovative Managers.

AMABILE, T. M. (1988) - *A Model of Creativity and Innovation in Organizations* - Research in Organizational Behavior, vol. 10.

ANDERSSON M. & LOOF H. (2009) - *Key characteristics of the small innovative firm* -
Cesis Electronic Working Paper Series.

ANSOFF I. (1975) - *Managing Strategic surprise by response to weak signals* - California Management Review, vol. 18.

AKRICH M. (1993) - *Les formes de la mediation technique* -

Reseaux, n° 60, July-August.
BALBONTIN et al (1999) - *New product development success factors in American and British firms* - International Journal of Technology Management, vol. 17.
BARDINI T. (2000) - *Les promesses de la revolution virtuelle : genese de l'informatique personnelle, 1968-1973* - Sociologie et societes, vol. 32.
BARNES L. (1961) - *Organizational Systems and Engineering Groups: A Comparative Study of Two Technical Groups in Industry* - Administrative Science Quarterly, vol. 6, n° 3.
BARON R. A. (2004) - *The cognitive perspective: a valuable tool for answering entrepreneurship's basic why questions* - Journal of Business Venturing, vol. 19.
BARON-COHEN S. (2002) - *The extreme male brain theory of autism* - Neurodevelopmental Disorders, MIT Press.
CASH J., EARL M. & MORISON R. (2008) - *Teaming Up to Crack Innovation Enterprise Integration* - Harvard Business School.
COLLINGS D. G, DONNELLAN B. & WHELAN E. (1997) - Managing talent in knowledge-intensive settings - Journal of Knowledge Management, vol. 14.
COX T. and BLAKE S. (1991) - *Managing Cultural Diversity: implications for organizational competitiveness* - Academy of Management Executive, vol. 5.
BOMSEL O. & LE BLANC G. (2000) - *Innovation et économie numerique* - Encyclopedie de l'innovation, Editions Economica.
CALLON M. (1986) - *Elements pour une sociologie de la traduction. La domestication des coquilles Saint-Jacques dans la Baie de Saint-Brieuc* - L'Annee sociologique, n°36.
FIOL M. (1996) - *Squeezing harder doesn't always work: continuing the search for consistency in innovation research* - The Academy of Management review.
HURLEY R. & HULT T. (1998) - *Innovation, Market Orientation, and Organizational Learning: An Integration and Empirical Examination* - Journal of Marketing.
JOYAL A. (1995) - *Le concept de milieu et les PME innovantes*

et exportatrices: etudes de cas le Quebec non-metropolitain - GREPME, Universite du Quebec a Trois-Rivieres.
KLINE S. & ROSENBERG N. (1986) - *An overwiew of innovation* - National Academies Press.
KOENING G. (1994) - *L'apprentissage organisationnel : reperage des lieux* - Revue francaise de gestion, n° 97.
LUBART T.I. & STERNBERG R.J. (1995) - *Ten tips toward creativity in the workplace* - Action in Organizations, Sage Publication.
MACKINNON D W. (1962) - *The nature and nurture of creative talent* - Amer. Psychol. vol. 17.
MALERBA F. & ORSENIGO L. (1993) - *Technological Regimes and Firm Behavior* - ICC
MULGAN G. & ALBURY D (2003)- *Innovation in the Public Sector* - Work awaiting publication.
O'REILLY C. A .& TUSHMAN M. L (1996) - *Ambidextrous organizations: Managing evolutionary and revolutionary change* - California Management Review, Summer 96, vol. 38.
LAPLANTE N. et al (2000) - *Innovation, organisation et relations de travail : une etude des processus de changement dans les services publiques* - Document de travail, Département de relations industrielles, Universite du Quebec a Hull.
LORINO P. (1998) - *Organisation et innovation : l'organisation a la franqaise* - Realites Industrielles, serie des Annales des Mines.
READ A. (2000) - *Determinants of successful organizational innovation: a review of current research* - Journal of Management Practice, vol. 3.
RHODES M. (1961) - *An analysis of creativity* - Phi Delta Kappan.
RICHARDSON G. B. (1978) - *The Organization of Industry* - Economic Journal, vol. 82.
RINGLAND G. (2006) - *Introduction to scenario planning* - Scenarios in Marketing.
RINGELMANN M. (1913) - *Recherches sur les moteurs*

animes: Travail de l'homme - Annales de l'Institut National Agronomique, 2nd series, vol. 12.

VAN DE VEN A. (1986) - *Central problems in the management of innovation* - School of Management, The University of Minnesota.

VERNON R. (1966) - *International investments and International trade in the product cycle* - The Quarterly Journal of Economics.

SCOTT R. & RUEF M. (1998) - *A Multidimensional Model of Organizational Legitimacy: Hospital Survival in Changing Institutional Environments* - Administrative Science Quarterly, vol. 43.

TAGGAR S. (2002) - *Individual Creativity and Group Ability to Utilize Individual Creative Resources: A Multilevel Model* - The Academy of Management Journal, vol. 45, n° 2.

TAYLOR W. et al (1958) - *Does Group Participation When Using Brainstorming Facilitate or Inhibit Creative Thinking?* - Administrative Science Quarterly, vol. 3, n° 1.

TAYON J. (2002) - *Is the Linux project a possible model for an innovative company?* - CNAM.

THOMKE S. H. (2001) - *The Essentials for Enlightened Experimentation* - Harvard Business Review Article.

Printed by Books on Demand GmbH, Norderstedt / Germany